WATER

WATER
The Next Great Resource Battle

LAURENCE PRINGLE

MACMILLAN PUBLISHING CO., INC. / New York
COLLIER MACMILLAN PUBLISHERS / London

c.1

PICTURE CREDITS: California Department of Water Resources, 104; Library of Congress, Farm and Security Administration (Arthur Rothstein), 64; Mobil Oil Corporation, 86; New York City Department of Environmental Protection, 22; *New York Times* Pictures (B. Vartan Boyajian), 48; Laurence Pringle, vi (both), 10, 13, 15, 26, 30, 32, 33, 38, 41, 42, 43, 45, 57, 59, 62, 92, 132; Standard Oil Co. (N. J.), 76; Cartoon by Bruce Stark, 120; Union Pacific Railroad Photo, 102; Official U.S. Coast Guard Photograph, 123; U.S. Department of Agriculture, 74 (Jim Pickerell), 77 (Fred Witte), 128, 129 (Soil Conservation Service); U.S. Department of the Interior, Bureau of Reclamation, 18 (B. D. Glaha), 78, 82 (W. L. Rusho), 90, 96, 98 (E. E. Hertzog), 109, 110, 111, 125; U.S. Department of the Interior, National Park Service Photo, 88 (Clare C. Ralston), 100 (Jack Rottier); U.S. Department of the Interior, Water and Power Resources Services, 108; Valmont Industries, Inc., 68. Maps and drawings by Harry Chester.

Macmillan Publishing Co., Inc.
866 Third Avenue, New York, N.Y. 10022
Collier Macmillan Canada, Inc.

Printed in the United States of America

10   9   8   7   6   5   4   3   2   1

Library of Congress Cataloging in Publication Data

Pringle, Laurence P.
Water: the next great resource battle.

(Science for survival series)
Bibliography: p.
Includes index.
SUMMARY: Explores the social, political, and economic aspects of a vital resource—water.
1. Water supply—United States—Juvenile literature.   2. Water consumption—United States—Juvenile literature.   [1. Water supply]   I. Title. II. Series.
TD223.P74   333.91'00973   81-23694
ISBN 0-02-775400-6   AACR2

Contents

Introduction

When the well's dry, we know the worth of water.
—Benjamin Franklin
Poor Richard's Almanack

The resource becomes scarce. There are local shortages, and people have to wait in line to replenish their supply. Prices soar, and up goes the cost of food and of countless other products made from the resource. People learn to get along with less, and they worry that someday there won't be enough of the resource to go around.

This resource could be gasoline or oil. It could also be water. Next to energy, no resource in the United States is attracting more attention and concern than water. There are many links between energy and water. Both affect our relations with other nations—with neighboring Canada and Mexico in the case of water. The cost of fuels affects the construction and operation

A reservoir during times of normal rainfall, and during a drought.

of reservoirs, irrigation systems, and other water projects, and whether farmers can afford to pump water from deep wells for their crops. So a lack of energy, or energy that is too costly, can limit water supplies.

On the other hand, water is needed for mining coal, making synthetic fuels, cooling power plants, generating hydroelectric power, and other energy projects. Lack of water may limit energy production. The two vital resources are intricately related.

Just as we once took cheap, plentiful energy for granted, we now take cheap, plentiful water for granted. We shouldn't. Droughts during the late 1970s caused regional water shortages and provided dramatic evidence of how much we depend upon water for basic necessities of life—drinking, keeping clean, raising food. In the arid West, drought speeded the depletion of precious, limited groundwater supplies. Water also ran short in areas where rainfall is abundant. We began to discover that supplies have been mismanaged and that even vast underground water reserves are threatened by pollution. Competition for water sharpened between states, between one part of a state and another, between long-time users and newcomers, between whites and Indians, between cities and irrigators.

Water supply has become a major national issue that, like energy, can have a great impact on our lives. This book explores the water resource of the United States—how we depend on it, how much we have, how we use and misuse it, and how we may be able to avoid creating a water crisis that rivals our troubles with energy.

WATER

Marathon runners must replenish the water they lose as they
perspire and exhale.

1. Water Is Life

In 1981, an Irishman in an English prison stopped eating and threatened to starve to death unless his political demands were met. The British government refused. The man continued his hunger strike, taking only water. On the sixty-sixth day of his fast, he died.

He was not the first person, nor the last, to deliberately starve for a cause he believed in. His story is mentioned here because it dramatically illustrates how we depend on water. People go on hunger strikes partly because they know that humans can survive for weeks without food. This allows time for publicity and political pressure to build, and perhaps to cause change. A protestor would be foolish to begin a food and *water* strike; he would be dead in a few days.

Water is the most important substance we consume. We *are* mostly water: A woman's body is 55 to 65 percent water, a man's 65 to 75 percent. Our blood is 83 percent water. Even our bones are 25 percent water. In our bodies, water makes food digestion possible. It carries hormones, nutrients, and disease-fighting cells to and from body organs. Water makes it possible for wastes to leave our bodies through urine, feces, skin, and lungs.

All this can be accomplished with about two and a half to three quarts of water a day. Take away this water and the chemical processes of life soon break down and stop.

We need not drink these vital three quarts of water directly, because we get water from other fluids, from foods, and from the digestion of proteins and other nutrients. Milk, orange juice, and apple juice are all about 88 percent water. Many foods are mostly water: The aptly named watermelon is 93 percent, yogurt is 89 percent, an apple 84 percent, and a banana 76 percent water. Even fried chicken and pizza are about half water. We are water eaters as well as water drinkers.

Before reaching us as food, a developing watermelon or chicken uses plenty of water, so our food represents much more water use than the actual water molecules that enter our bodies. A person living on bread alone, for instance, would actually use 300 gallons of water per day—the amount needed to grow the wheat for two and a half pounds of bread. About 120 gallons of water are needed to produce one egg. An eight-ounce serving of beefsteak represents the consumption of an estimated 3,500 gallons. The steer from which the steak came may drink only twelve gallons a day, but the alfalfa or other forage it eats consumes enormous amounts of water. According to a University of California study, more than 4,500 gallons of water are needed to produce three meals a day for one person.

People seldom think of this indirect water use. We are conscious only of the water we use directly. Drinking and cooking account for two gallons a day. In the average American home, each person uses an additional eighty-five gallons daily: twenty-four for flushing toilets, thirty-two for bathing, dishwashing, and laundry, and twenty-five for such uses as gardens, lawns, car washing, and swimming pools.

12

Including the water needed to grow grain fed to chickens, about 1,440 gallons are needed to produce a dozen eggs.

The total—eighty-seven gallons a day for each person—is an estimate. Other assessments put the average consumption in America much higher, up to 175 gallons a day. There is agreement, however, that water use varies widely around the nation. It is much higher in regions where intensive lawn watering is practiced. In such places, direct water use by each person may exceed 300 gallons a day.

Directly and indirectly, people in the United States use 700 billion gallons of water each day—eighteen times the amount used in 1900. Population growth alone doesn't account for this great increase. Modern plumbing, in shower heads and flush toilets, for instance, has been designed to use more water than necessary. The use of water for industrial cooling and especially for large-scale irrigation has added greatly to the nation's thirst.

We use a lot of water and will need more as the population grows and as we develop coal and other domestic energy resources. Does a national water crisis lie ahead? Will we run out of water? If we do, it will be a result of greed, folly, and mismanagement, not a lack of water, for our water resources are incredibly plentiful.

OUR WATERY WORLD

Although some comparisons between our water and energy resources are valid, there is a basic difference between water and such common energy sources as oil, coal, and natural gas. When these fossil fuels are burned, the earth's supply is depleted. (As they burn, incidentally, some water vapor is released.) They are nonrenewable resources. Some day they will be scarce and extremely expensive.

The use of water does not diminish the world's supply. None is lost, and the supply is great. The total amount of water on earth is about 326 cubic miles. (One cubic mile equals about a trillion gallons.) This total includes water as solid ice in glaciers and polar icecaps, as vapor in the earth's atmosphere, and as liquid in the oceans, lakes, rivers, soils, and rocks. More than 99 percent of the earth's water is either brine in oceans and seas or ice in glaciers and icecaps.

Dr. Raymond L. Nace, a research hydrologist with the United States Geological Survey, pictured the earth's water supply this way: "If the total amount of water in existence is considered as one barrel of fifty-five gallons, then the ocean

For drinking, bathing, and such uses as swimming pools, we usually take abundant, inexpensive fresh water for granted.

represents fifty gallons. Icecaps and glaciers would be a small block of ice equal to about one gallon. The remaining water would be in a four-gallon bucket representing all water in the atmosphere, lakes and inland seas, groundwater reservoirs, and soil moisture."

Fresh water is only a small part of all water, but even this resource is enormous. Each day the sun evaporates a trillion tons of water from the oceans and continents and pumps it as vapor into the atmosphere. Each day the same amount of water vapor condenses and falls as rain, hail, sleet, or snow. Much of this fresh water falls into the oceans, but 4.2 trillion gallons of precipitation fall on the continental United States each day.

According to the United States Water Resources Council, more than half of this water—2,787 billion gallons—evaporates into the atmosphere. Rivers and streams carry another 1,328 billion gallons to the oceans or to Canada and Mexico. Each day about 61 billion gallons soak into the ground. This ground-

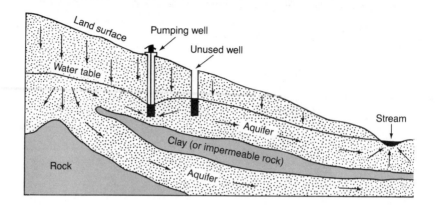

water may be tapped by wells. It supplies about half of the water used by people.

Groundwater and surface water are not separate. One replenishes the other. The top of groundwater, called the water table, is usually underground, but in valleys and other low places it reaches the surface and contributes to the water in lakes, ponds, swamps, and marshes. This is especially true when there is little surface runoff from rain or melted snow. At such times about 30 percent of the water we see in rivers and other streams comes from groundwater. So groundwater is a vital part of the fresh-water resources of the United States.

Some people imagine that some groundwater flows in huge underground rivers or exists in cavernous lakes. In fact, large amounts of water do collect in underground storage areas, but they are formations of porous rocks, loose sands, gravels, and soils. These water-saturated formations are called aquifers. They may be thick or thin, big or small, deep or shallow.

The size and shape of aquifers are affected by formations of rocks or clay that block the movement of water underground. Sometimes these nonporous materials are arranged in layers, with an aquifer between the layers. Some aquifers are enclosed in a sort of underground basin by nonporous rocks, so their water doesn't go anywhere. In aquifers with outlets, the water moves, from a few feet to a few hundred feet a year. Aquifers near coasts often release tremendous amounts of fresh water into bays and other estuaries at the ocean's edge.

Of the total fresh water on the surface and underground, only about 5 percent is used by people. This seems to make talk of water shortages silly. But the talk is serious and the threat of severe regional water shortages is real. Vast amounts of fresh water in rivers and lakes are unfit for use by people. The water is contaminated with industrial wastes, human wastes, pesticides, and a variety of other pollutants. There are growing numbers of reports of polluted well water, too.

Furthermore, the nation's rain and snow do not fall evenly across the land. Although the national average is thirty inches of annual precipitation, states east of the Mississippi River receive about forty inches or more. That's about a million gallons an acre. Parts of the Pacific Northwest receive eighty inches, but most of the West is water-poor. Eastern Nebraska receives twenty-seven inches, but the western part of the state gets only eighteen. Fourteen inches of precipitation fall on Wyoming, whereas Nevada, the driest state, gets just nine inches. Overall, the West, with 60 percent of the nation's land, gets only a quarter of its precipitation.

Scarcity of water has long been a fact of life for westerners. It has resulted in water laws that are different from those in the East, and in the building of huge dams and other projects for storing and moving water. Conditions in the arid West are dramatically different from those in water-rich areas. Yet both Nevada (with nine inches of rain annually) and New Jersey (with forty-five inches) face water supply problems.

Water-rich or water-poor, people all over the United States can no longer take dependable supplies of clean water for granted.

2. Drought in Waterland

The United States has no national water policy. The authority to provide water and to plan for future needs has been left to state, city, and county governments, which in turn oversee or operate a total of 50,000 public or private water companies. The federal government does play a big role in water management, though, especially in the West. It has provided many billions of dollars for dams, irrigation canals, and similar projects. Sixteen federal agencies have programs that influence water use, development, and quality. They sometimes work at cross-purposes, and this contributes to fragmented, haphazard water management in the United States.

At certain times and places, water is like the air: It doesn't belong to anyone in particular, and it can be used or abused freely. At other times, water is owned: for example, when it is in a water company reservoir or when a property owner in the West has rights to a certain amount of water each year. In either case, water is a form of wealth. People who use the

A 1934 photograph of the Hoover Dam under construction on the Colorado River.

water are usually determined to continue. So water management is often more of a political or economic problem than an engineering problem. Most water supply difficulties are complex and cannot be solved quickly. This is revealed most dramatically by some examples from the water-rich eastern United States.

For decades, water supply troubles have been developing in the nation's oldest cities, mostly in the East. Many water distribution systems and sewer lines were laid in the 1800s and early 1900s. The pipes, valves, tunnels, and other parts of these systems had a life expectancy of fifty to seventy-five years. Needed modernization was delayed by the Depression of the 1930s and later by World War II. Since then, the financial problems of cities have worsened, and so has the condition of such basic structures and services as streets, bridges, sewers, mass transit, and water systems.

Many older cities have water pipes made of cast iron that have weakened over the years. Boston, which began laying its water system in the 1840s, has about 1,100 miles of water pipes now. Most of the system is old, but the city can only afford to replace about 1 percent of it each year. The system carries 150 million gallons a day, but loses at least 20 percent through leaks. The loss is difficult to measure, since some buildings are unmetered and many existing meters don't work. According to a Washington research organization called the Urban Institute, Pittsburgh loses 14 percent of its water by leakage, Philadelphia 12 percent, and Baltimore 10 percent.

Inadequate sewer systems also affect drinking water supplies. Surface runoff of rainwater mixes with sewage in many cities. The great volume of water overwhelms sewage treatment plants, adding untreated wastes to lakes and rivers from which water supplies are drawn. Breakdowns of sewer and water systems are becoming more common.

New York shares these problems with many other cities. Forty percent of its water pipes are more than sixty years old. A special threat to the dependability of the city's water supply involves tunnels that bring water to the city. In the mid-1880s, some farsighted planners decided to reach to hills and mountains north of the city for its water supply. The system was later expanded even farther upstate. Now some of New York's water comes from 125 miles away. Much of it flows by gravity from reservoirs in the Catskill Mountains, which include the beginnings of the Delaware River. The quality of New York's water is exceptional, for it lacks the highly chlorinated flavor of most "city water."

Aqueducts bring the water to a reservoir near the city. From there it is sent into the city via two tunnels cut through rock hundreds of feet below ground. Up to seventeen feet wide, the tunnels carry a river of 1.5 billion gallons into the city each day for further distribution to 800,000 commercial and residential buildings.

This is 60 percent more water than the tunnels, built in 1917 and 1936, were designed to carry. Their inside surfaces have never been inspected because large sections are inaccessible while in use. There is evidence that the tunnels have deteriorated and need repair. However, engineers have not even tested the giant valves that would play a key role in controlling the flow of water, in the event of a tunnel breakdown. The valves are so old that they might not reopen after being closed.

There is danger of a major breakdown of New York City's water system—one that would leave millions of people without water for weeks or months. This problem was recognized in the 1950s, and a third water tunnel was planned. Once it was in operation, the other tunnels could be repaired, one at a time. Construction began in 1970, and the sixty-mile tunnel was supposed to be finished in 1977. By 1981, however, only

21

New York City officials emerge from a tour of the vital but
incomplete third water tunnel.

eleven miles had been completed, still not enough for parts
of the older tunnels to be taken out of service for repair.

New York City could not afford the billions of dollars needed
to complete this vital water tunnel. Some of New York's
political representatives argued that funds from the federal
government were needed, and deserved. For decades, most
federal funds for water projects went to the South and the
West. In 1978, for example, the amount of federal money given
to Idaho for water projects equaled $76.88 for each state resi-
dent. In contrast, the per-capita share in New York was just
15 cents. In Washington, a coalition of senators and representatives from the Northeast and the Midwest tried to bring more
federal water-resources funds to their regions.

About the public money spent on western water projects,

Mayor Edward Koch of New York City said, "They have these multiple-purpose projects out there that combine irrigation, flood control, and recreation—so they make out like bandits. Well, we can't have water-skiing in our city tunnels. If I could figure out a way to put canoeists down there, maybe our problems would be solved."

Struggling along with antiquated, poorly maintained water systems, many older cities also face a rising demand for water. New York City's population has declined, but its water use has risen—from 177 gallons a day for each resident in 1970 to 190 gallons in 1980. The increased use of washing machines, dishwashers, and air conditioners accounted for much of this rising demand.

Northern New Jersey had little population growth during the 1970s, but people living there increased their use of water. New industry, plus a sports complex that used 500,000 gallons a day, also added to the strain on existing water systems. Generally, the greatest water use is found in regions of new development. New residential areas use lots of water to start lawns and shrubs.

In 1975, when rainfall was plentiful and reservoirs were full in the Northeast, a study conducted by the United States Army Corps of Engineers warned that the gap between supply and demand for water was narrowing. The report urged that steps be taken to increase supply or reduce consumption. Otherwise, the report predicted, the next drought would cause shortages from Virginia to New England.

There were other warnings. A 1975 study of New Jersey's water supply predicted a severe shortage by 1985 unless certain steps were taken—the first one being construction of an aqueduct from two reservoirs in the Raritan River Basin to a reservoir near Newark. According to Dr. Robert M. Hordon, a professor of geography at Rutgers College, "The yield from the Raritan Basin is in surplus of 70 million gallons a day, but it is not allotted to anyone. It is just sitting there and, as of now, there is no way to get it out—the ultimate in planning."

The New Jersey study did not advocate any major new water projects, concluding that water needs could be met by reducing consumption and pollution and by better cooperation among the 178 different water companies that serve northeastern and central New Jersey. (In all, the state has 600 water companies.) This situation—"probably the most politically fragmented water-supply system of any metropolitan region in the world"—was judged to be the main obstacle to a more secure water supply for the state's 7.3 million residents.

Connecticut had similar problems. Its water supply varies greatly from community to community—a result not of rainfall but of the way the water companies manage the available water. Connecticut's 395 water companies vary greatly in their foresightedness, prosperity, and other characteristics. The state government interfered very little in water planning, even though studies showed that water reserves weren't adequate.

Throughout the East there is no scarcity of water, but rather a scarcity of *deliverable* water in certain places at certain times. Lack of money has prevented the construction of new reservoirs, aqueducts, and other storage and delivery facilities. In the densely settled East, river valleys and other appropriate sites for new reservoirs are also valued for farming or recreation, so there is often strong opposition to new water projects. People's attitudes toward water also add to the difficulties. "It is like the man who does not get around to repairing the roof until it rains," said Robert Sprangler, a spokesman for the American Waterworks Association. "When those reservoirs are full, people don't think about putting their money there."

DROUGHT IN WATERLAND

Drought struck in 1980 and extended into 1981. The troubles that many had predicted came true. Throughout the East, some areas had adequate water supplies, while other, neighboring communities were forced to ration water. Water rationing was imposed on the 3.5 million residents of southern Florida. In Massachusetts, lack of water caused the state university at Amherst to close for a few days, as a result of poor planning by the local water company. Years of warning had had no effect. Charles Lacey, director of the community's water conservation program, said, "We're a small town with small reservoirs, and if it doesn't rain for six weeks, they go dry. We've been gambling every year since the university started expanding."

The effects of drought touched off a water battle between two neighboring Virginia cities. Norfolk, on Chesapeake Bay, relies on Suffolk for most of its water. Decades ago, Norfolk bought land and built reservoirs in Suffolk, which is largely undeveloped land, with many peanut farms. These reservoirs served 690,000 people in Norfolk and Virginia Beach. When drought lowered water levels to a hundred-day supply, Norfolk took steps to conserve. Firefighters used salt water rather than fresh water. And water rates rose sharply for anyone who used more than 75 percent of the previous year's average consumption.

Norfolk also sought to drill emergency wells on land it owned in Suffolk. The Suffolk City Council voted to block the drilling. Suffolk residents resent the fact that reservoir water from their lands goes elsewhere, while they depend on wells to supply their needs. Suffolk farmers feared that Norfolk's new wells would cause their smaller wells to dry up.

Norfolk officials argued that the wells would be used only

Coastal Norfolk, Virginia, depends on inland reservoirs for
its supply of fresh water.

for emergencies. And one official called Suffolk the "Saudi
Arabia of water," referring to its abundant groundwater supply. Beneath Suffolk lies part of the Potomac aquifer, which
hydrologists say holds an immense supply of water. Troubles
between the cities eased by mid-1981, when heavy rains replenished the reservoirs. The wells were no longer needed, but
the longstanding feud between the cities seemed likely to
erupt again, probably with the next drought.

During the 1980–1981 drought, the New Jersey government
set limits on water use in the densely populated northeastern

part of the state. A combination of water meters and computers enabled one large water company to quickly identify the industries, offices, and homes that were exceeding water rationing limits. Millions of dollars in fines were levied against violators.

New York City's water saving program had to rely mostly on voluntary cooperation because its homes and apartment buildings lack water meters. This characteristic of New York's, plus the city's heavy consumption of water, stirred up resentment in other states. New York has rights to much of the water from the Delaware River headwaters in the western Catskill Mountains. This arrangement has never pleased others, including residents and businesses in Pennsylvania, New Jersey, and Delaware who are dependent on the 280-mile river. A four-state agency, the Delaware River Basin Commission, regulates the use of the river and its tributaries.

Philadelphia's water commissioner pointed out that New Yorkers use their water just once, then flush or drain it into the Atlantic Ocean. In contrast, people who use water directly from the Delaware and its tributaries use the water several times before it reaches the sea. In scores of Pennsylvania and New Jersey communities, water used in homes and for some industrial purposes is processed in sewage treatment plants, returned to the river, and later drawn into water purification plants in downstream cities. This reuse of water is common in the United States. One-third of the population uses water containing one gallon of treated waste water for every thirty gallons of flow. Usually the waste water emerged only hours before from an upstream sewer.

New York City officials acknowledged that no water was recycled there, but said that this was simply a result of geography, since the city is by the ocean. Before the drought eased, however, New York was required to reduce its use of water from the Delaware watershed (the region from which the river's water drains). This maintained enough water in the river to help dilute pollution and to keep salt water from extending far upstream of Delaware Bay.

Rainfall returned to nearly normal in most of the East during 1981. The drought eased. Restrictions on water use ended in most communities. Ironically, in northern New Jersey, rationing was still in effect in some areas when two reservoirs filled to the brim and began losing water to rivers and thence to the ocean. The Boontown Reservoir lost nearly 2 billion gallons in three days. No aqueducts connected overflowing reservoirs with others in the region that were still well below capacity. This showed again that New Jersey was not short of water but lacked sound planning and cooperation among water companies.

Once rationing ended, many people began to waste water again. Images of a real water crisis—with people lined up to fill jugs from tank trucks, and trench toilets dug outdoors—faded from the public's consciousness. Such a crisis remains a real possibility, however, and solutions to the problem of more dependable water supplies are being sought.

READY FOR THE NEXT DROUGHT?

At the request of New York State's Department of Environmental Conservation, the U.S. Geological Survey began a study of the Brooklyn-Queens aquifer—a groundwater source that lies beneath two boroughs of New York City. The aquifer once supplied much of the water for Brooklyn and Queens. It may reach as deep as 1,000 feet, and extends right to the surface. In fact, water from the aquifer sometimes floods basements.

This aquifer is believed to hold 1,500 billion gallons—more than three times the amount in all the New York City reservoirs. But there are unknowns about this resource, the foremost of which is its quality. By 1982, a geological survey had found that parts of the aquifer were contaminated by salt from the ocean and by nitrates from fertilizers and leaky sewer lines. Some of the aquifer water may be potable; the rest might be used for nondrinking purposes, freeing the city's high quality tap water for vital uses.

Another solution to New York City's water problems, first proposed in 1975, called for taking water from the Hudson River. This river, the thirty-first largest in the nation, flows past New York and would seem to be an obvious source. But the river is an estuary, with salty water reaching many miles upstream. Furthermore, it is badly polluted before it reaches the city and, once there, receives millions of gallons of untreated human wastes daily.

In 1977, the Army Corps of Engineers proposed a Hudson River project designed to avoid these problems. At times of high flow, nearly a billion gallons a day would be taken from the Hudson at a point eighty-five miles upstream from the tip of Manhattan. Pumped through a tunnel to a treatment plant, the water would then flow by gravity to a reservoir near New York. There it would be mixed with supplies from the existing city system. The plan also called for linking the city's system with that of Nassau County, Long Island, an area dependent on groundwater that may become too polluted for use. To allay fears about pollutants in Hudson River water, the Corps of Engineers pointed out that people in several mid-Hudson cities already used river water for drinking without ill effects. The cost of the project was estimated at nearly $5 billion.

The proposal was met by a flood of criticism, first from private environmental groups, then from the state Department of Environmental Conservation and the U.S. Environmental Protection Agency. The idea of mixing the city's water with

29

In the Hudson Highlands, 40 miles inland from New York City, the river's water is still too salty for human consumption.

Hudson River water, even after treatment, appalled many people. As one editorial writer put it, "To add Hudson River water to New York's present supply is to degrade one of the few city assets that have remained in prime condition over the years. It would be like diluting champagne with root beer."

The Corps of Engineers proposal was also criticized because it ignored or underestimated alternatives. One environmental group described the project as a "traditional Corps response to water supply problems, focusing single-mindedly on massive, costly structural projects with tendencies towards cost overruns." This has been called "the old billion-dollar boon-doggle approach to water resource management."

Critics of the Corps plan said that it underestimated the potential of water conservation measures in New York City that would make the project unnecessary. The Corps estimated that just 5.4 percent of the city's water demand could be reduced by conservation. Others contended that a vigorous conservation program could reduce water use by 20 percent in the city.

In addition to campaigns aimed at increasing voluntary reduction of water use, this program would include plugging leaks and metering water. Leakage from underground pipes in New York City is estimated at anywhere from 8.5 to 15 percent of the supply. In 1981, the city spent $5 million reducing other, easy-to-reach leaks—in fire hydrants and in thousands of abandoned buildings.

For water metering to be effective, every apartment should have a meter, with water rates then set to discourage heavy use. But installing water meters in individual apartments in New York would be a huge, expensive task (though much less costly than the proposed Hudson River project). A first step, considered by the City Council, was to require individual water meters in all new multifamily buildings and in buildings that were being renovated.

Voluntary conservation of water is a key element in any water saving program, and there is disagreement about how effective this can be. During the 1980–1981 drought, people in Greenwich, Connecticut, offered some idea of the potential savings by conservation. Greenwich was the eastern city that came closest to running out of water, at one time having just a nineteen-day supply. Residents and businesses cut water use by 25 percent, with some achieving a 45-percent reduction. People were inconvenienced, drove dirty cars, and were per-

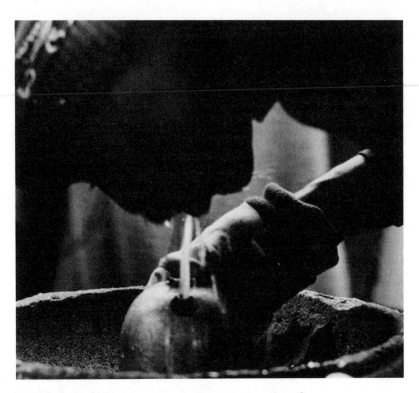

New York City's fine water is one of its greatest assets, but
the distribution system is badly in need of repair.

haps somewhat dirtier than usual themselves, but they had
water for all essential uses. Several months after the water
emergency ended, people continued to practice some water
conservation, though total use crept back to within 10 percent
of previous levels. The question remains: Will people volun-
tarily save significant amounts of water all the time, not just
during an emergency?

As cities and other communities in the East looked at their
water supplies for the 1980s and beyond, it was clear that
some structural changes were needed, such as new reservoirs,
and aqueducts connecting water companies. But if increased

Poor maintenance of water systems allows waste of precious water.

water supplies are managed no better than before, these improvements will also fail to provide dependable water supplies. One example of water-management-as-usual: Many water companies in the East still charge customers a lower rate when they use greater volumes of water—an invitation to waste water.

In 1980, the United States Water Resources Council (set up to advise federal agencies on water problems) said of the Northeast, "The region's water problems are probably the most diverse, complex, and unique conflict of demands, institutional arrangements, and feasibility of solutions" of any in the nation. In an area that is rich with water, economic and political obstacles still threaten to cause troublesome and perhaps disastrous shortages.

Pollution of rivers and lakes has been reduced somewhat, but the quality of drinking water has declined.

3. Chemical Cocktails

During the drought that extended into 1981, the Passaic River in northeastern New Jersey dropped so low that up to 70 percent of its water came from sewage treatment plants. Yet more than 2 million people continued to use the river for drinking water. At the main water treatment plant, the amount of chlorine added to the water was increased 300 percent. According to the plant superintendent, the water was safe to drink. "There's no health problem at all," he said. "The amount of chlorine we use is more than adequate to kill bacteria and viruses. There isn't a thing that could get through."

He was correct in one sense: Chlorination of water kills the bacteria that cause such diseases as typhoid fever, cholera, and diphtheria. But chlorine has little effect on viruses and none at all on pesticides, herbicides, fertilizers, lead, cadmium, and scores of other chemicals that routinely *do* get through water treatment plants and eventually flow out of faucets. Any assessment of deliverable water supplies has to take their quality into account, since a contaminated source is about as good as no source (though it may have uses other than for drinking and cooking).

In the early 1970s, the United States began a major effort

35

to reduce water pollution. The Federal Water Pollution Control Act of 1972 set a goal of making all of the country's rivers and lakes "fishable and swimmable" by 1983. After ten years and the expenditure of more than $30 billion in federal and state funds, it was apparent that this goal would not be met. To accomplish it, at least $100 billion more would be needed.

New sewage treatment plants and other pollution control facilities had done some good, however. Nationally, the volume of waste emptied into rivers, streams, and lakes had been reduced. In many places, surface waters and tap water looked and smelled better. But the emphasis had been on surface waters, not underground supplies, and half of the United States population depends on well water. Furthermore, though it was hard to find any harmful bacteria in drinking water, other pollutants were often present. The emphasis on cleaning up rivers and lakes inadvertently distracted attention from a more vital task—safeguarding the water that people use daily for drinking, cooking, and bathing.

In the 1970s, studies of community water supplies all over the country revealed potentially harmful chemicals. The tap water of New Orleans, taken mostly from the Mississippi River before being treated, contained sixty-six chemical pollutants, including two known to cause cancer. Tests of drinking water from seventy-nine other cities, including Philadelphia, St. Louis, Kansas City, and San Francisco, revealed that all had at least six chemical pollutants.

More than 350 synthetic organic chemicals have been found in the nation's drinking water. (Organic chemicals contain carbon compounds and include such chemical families as alcohols, ethers, esters, aldehydes, amines, and chlorides.) Over fifty of these chemicals have been identified as "known or potential causes of cancer" by the International Agency for Research on Cancer.

Often the amounts of these chemicals are small—from 0.01 to 5.0 parts per billion. Water analyzing devices have become more sophisticated, allowing chemists to detect impurities that previously could not be measured. There was disagreement about the hazard to people from the minute amounts of chemicals found. In the view of many water company engineers and even of some state health departments, the hazard was doubtful and not proved.

To other health officials and to some environmental groups, the evidence was strong enough to warrant action. There was, for example, a high incidence of stomach and intestinal cancers found among people who drink water from the Lower Mississippi River. And there was the possibility that ingesting small to moderate amounts of the chemicals in water could eventually cause other illness, even if there was no clear link between cause and effect. A conservative approach to this health issue was that no substance capable of causing cancer, organ damage, birth defects, or other serious harm should remain in drinking water if a feasible way of removing it was available —or if the substance could be kept out of water in the first place.

"Nobody knows exactly what the risk is," said Dr. Nancy Kim of the New York Department of Health. "These chemicals don't belong in drinking water. Our policy is that they should be kept at a minimum. But if I have to prove they're a danger to humans, I can't, because the data [are] not there."

In 1977, the National Research Council, part of the National Academy of Sciences, reported on studies of some chemical contaminants found in drinking water. Twenty-two were known or suspected carcinogens (cancer-causing substances). Others were known to cause birth defects, to damage genetic materials in cells, or to harm the heart, liver, kidneys, or other organs. For some of these chemicals, the National Research

Tap water in the United States is free of harmful bacteria, but usually contains small amounts of chemical impurities.

Council was able to recommend "acceptable daily intake levels," but the information about a larger number was too scanty to set standards that were known to be safe. The report urged that research be conducted to learn more about these compounds. It concluded that although there was no evidence that at common levels found in water any of the substances caused cancer, an "abundance of uncertainties" dictated caution.

A FLOOD OF IMPURITIES

No one drinks pure water, unless it has been purified in a laboratory. Rain from the sky or water from underground aquifers contains impurities, though not necessarily harmful ones. Water from mineral springs often has nutrients that humans need daily—calcium, potassium, and magnesium, for example. Some natural impurities are harmful. Groundwater in parts of North Carolina and several other states has dangerous levels of radioactive radium. In parts of Mississippi the abundant groundwater has high levels of iron and is highly acidic and corrosive. In wilderness desert areas, some springs naturally contain lethal amounts of minerals. And in northwestern Pennsylvania, an outbreak of an intestinal disorder was traced to a protozoan from the droppings of beavers that lived upstream from local reservoirs.

People have never had water of absolute purity, but today's drinking water is sometimes a chemical cocktail of several compounds formerly not found in water. It is important to know the sources of these impurities and how they reach water supplies. Since the early 1940s, more and more chemical compounds have been marketed, used, and discarded into the environment. In 1941, the United States petrochemical industry produced a billion pounds of compounds. In 1977, production was 350 billion pounds. The production wastes alone from this output pose an enormous disposal problem.

Other industries produce chemical wastes, and there are an estimated 2,000 abandoned toxic-waste dumps scattered across the nation. Many of them are releasing known poisonous substances, as well as potentially harmful ones, into the ground and eventually into water supplies. Of these chemicals, Eckhardt C. Beck, assistant administrator of the Environmental Protection Agency's Office of Water and Waste Management, said in 1980, "These chemical contaminants frequently have multisyllabic, technical names. They sound foreign to our ears. They seem foreign to our lives. But that doesn't prevent them coming through the kitchen faucet."

It isn't difficult to imagine how other pollutants reach water supplies, whether in lakes and rivers or underground.

39

Even as raindrops fall through the air, they may pick up lead from automobile exhaust or sulfur dioxide from coal-burning power plants. Water that soaks into the ground carries substances from the surface. They may include fertilizers, herbicides, and pesticides from farmland, gardens, and lawns, and oil, lead, and cadmium from highway surfaces. Much of the rain that falls in cities and suburbs cannot soak easily into the ground. It runs off roofs, parking lots, driveways, and streets and is then carried through sewers to lakes, rivers, or other surface waters.

Tremendous amounts of pollutants are carried by storm runoff. A study in Milwaukee, Wisconsin, showed that an estimated 5,400 pounds of lead, 7,600 pounds of zinc, 2,100 pounds of copper, 170 pounds of chromium, and 12 pounds of polychlorinated biphenyls (PCBs) are found on paved surfaces in that city, ready to be washed away by rain or melting snow. In any city, rain also washes such organic materials as garbage and dog droppings into surface waters.

Most urban areas have not begun to deal effectively with the problem of storm runoff. Impurities can be reduced by improved street sweeping (especially with vacuum sweepers), frequent catch-basin cleaning, and the storage of runoff water for later treatment. Detroit, Seattle, and a few other cities have a large enough capacity in their sewer systems to store runoff until it can be passed through a treatment plant. Chicago is building 200- to 300-foot underground caverns to store runoff water.

The rapid runoff of rainwater in urban and suburban areas may have other effects on water supplies. When less water soaks into the ground, the water table drops, and this may cause wells to run dry. (Considering the quality of the groundwater in some areas, a dry well may be a blessing.) In coastal regions, a decline in groundwater often upsets the balance

As raindrops fall, they pick up airborne pollutants.

between fresh water and salt water. As fresh water declines, salt water from the ocean moves inland. Instead of running dry, a well may produce water that is too salty for drinking.

High concentrations of salt can also be found in some water supplies far from oceans, in northern Snow Belt states. The source is salts that are spread on highways. (The salts are often a combination of calcium chloride and sodium chloride.) Salt lowers the freezing point of water and causes ice and snow to melt and run off road surfaces. About 9 million tons—10 percent of all salt produced on earth—is spread on roads in the United States each year.

The direct cost of the salts and their application is $200 million. There are other, indirect costs. Roadside soils sometimes have fifty-five times more sodium and twenty-four times more chloride than normal. This affects plants in much the same way as drought. It stunts their growth, causes leaves to die, and sometimes kills trees and other vegetation. Salt also corrodes underground water pipes, telephone cables, electric lines, and such metal structures as bridges. It corrodes automobiles and hastens their depreciation.

Salt in storm runoff reaches rivers and other surface waters, where it is diluted but may still have harmful effects. Up to half of the salts used on roads and streets enters groundwater and then public and private wells, where it becomes a potential health hazard. Excessive intake of salts can contribute to high

41

Increasing numbers of wells have been contaminated by salt used to melt ice and snow from streets and highways.

blood pressure (hypertension). According to medical authorities, millions of Americans should reduce their salt intake; some are already on low-salt or salt-free diets prescribed by their doctors.

Physicians in New England and other northern regions have been urged to alert their patients to possible high salt levels in drinking water. About 27 percent of Massachusetts's drinking water supplies are contaminated with road salts, and some wells have had to be abandoned. Lawsuits were filed against the state government for its salting practices. Nevertheless, the idea of reducing the use of salts on roads is strongly resisted. Highway maintenance engineers see little chance of change. "What do you want, highways or skating rinks?" asked a Massachusetts highway official. "Salt's the only way to keep the roads going."

This attitude is supported by the salt industry, which states that salt makes winter driving much safer. There is little evidence to support this claim. Salt does produce a snow-free road more quickly than sand or cinders put on the surface. Thus it is an aid to faster driving, but not necessarily to safety.

Water running off streets, sidewalks, and other surfaces carries impurities into rivers and lakes, and also into groundwater.

Some communities have reduced their road salting without ill effects. Over a span of several years, Monroe County in western New York gradually cut its use of salt from 141,000 tons a year to 28,000 tons. Traffic accidents increased in the wintertime, but they increased similarly in the summer, the result of a general rise in traffic volume. Tests of well water revealed that salt concentrations had dropped.

NEW WAYS TO CLEAN WATER

Concern about chemical impurities in water supplies caused Congress to pass the Safe Drinking Water Act of 1974. This law empowered the Environmental Protection Agency (EPA),

43

in 1977, to begin regulating the nation's 40,000 community water systems and 200,000 smaller ones run by such establishments as hotels and housing developments. The initial goal of regulation was to ensure that water companies test their supplies more frequently and thoroughly than before. The EPA also set upper limits on six pesticides and ten other harmful chemicals found in drinking water.

Feeling federal regulation for the first time, the water companies did not respond well to the EPA standards. Individually and through the American Waterworks Association (AWA), they boasted of the quality of their water, resisted change, and questioned the data upon which the new safety standards had been established. They also objected to the cost of complying with the regulations, estimated by the EPA to be up to $2 billion over a five-year period.

An environmentalist described those who opposed stricter water safety standards as "a group of nineteenth-century-minded engineers and public health officials whose only knowledge and concern is about waterborne diseases caused by bacteria."

Methods of treating water have not changed for decades in the United States, even though water content has changed. Customers of many public water systems drink partly used water; only hours before, some of it was discharged from a municipal or industrial sewer. When such water is taken into a complete treatment plant, it is first disinfected with chlorine. Various chemicals are added to coagulate minerals and to neutralize unpleasant tastes and smells. Then more chemicals are added in order to remove the corrective ones. The water is then filtered through sand and chlorinated to prevent contamination as the water is distributed through the community's system.

Chlorination kills bacteria but not many of the hundred

A water company employee adjusts a chlorinating device. Chlorination was once thought to be a cure-all for water health risks.

types of viruses that can be waterborne. Other processes at treatment plants remove some but not all viruses. So far, the only known way to eliminate them all is to boil the water. (High concentrations of viruses have been known to cause epidemics, but the low concentrations normally found in drinking water may yet be linked with much of the chronic ill health in the United States.) Chlorine has also been ineffective against outbreaks of giardiasis, an intestinal illness caused by a parasitic protozoan, in Pennsylvania, Oregon, Colorado, and California. The chlorination process, therefore, is not the panacea it is often thought to be. Furthermore, in 1974 it was discovered that chlorine, reacting with dead algae and other organic materials in water, produces a group of chemicals called trihalomethanes (THMs). One THM chloroform—causes cancer in laboratory rodents. In 1977, the EPA set the THM limit for drinking water at a hundred parts per billion.

Water companies found the matter of THMs particularly troubling since it challenged their decades-old "cure-all,"

45

chlorination. The federal THM limit was challenged in court by the AWA, which claimed that the regulation was unnecessary and costly. A group of water companies proposed that the THM limit be set at 300 parts per billion. This happened to be a little less than the highest recorded concentration in the country, so very few water companies would have had to change their ways of treating water.

According to Dr. Erwin Bellack of the EPA's Office of Drinking Water, the THM standard was chosen, not because it was known to be safe, but because it was known to be attainable. The agency's general policy was to limit human exposure to carcinogens to the maximum extent possible. Thus, if better methods for limiting THMs in water were developed, the EPA would set a stricter standard for these chemicals.

In 1981, new studies reported by the President's Council on Environmental Quality appeared to strengthen the evidence linking water chlorination and cancer. The report concluded that people who drink chlorinated surface water bear a greater risk of developing rectal, colon, or bladder cancer than people who drink well water, chlorinated or not. (Presumably, well water contains little organic matter with which chlorine can react to form THMs.)

Nevertheless, in view of chlorine's effectiveness against most waterborne diseases, health experts urged caution about changing water treatment methods. Water suppliers had several ways to reduce THM levels. Simply using less chlorine was possible in some cases. Another method was to use filters of granular activated carbon to remove THMs or to remove organic materials before chlorine could react with them. Such filters are used by many European cities. They are made of a porous form of carbon that presents an enormous surface area to contaminants. A single pound of tiny carbon granules exposes more than 4 million square feet of surface to which organic chemicals can adhere. "Activated" carbon is carbon that has been altered in ways that make it chemically "sticky," so that many molecules can adhere as water flows through. The carbon has to be replaced occasionally; the more pollutants in the water, the more often it must be replaced.

According to the EPA, the cost of such filters for large water companies would add just four to seven dollars a year to water bills for a family of four. Water companies claimed that the cost would be much higher.

Filters of substances other than carbon were under investigation as well. Chemical substitutes for chlorine were also studied. One was called Agent 1. Preliminary tests with Agent 1 showed that it was less likely to react with organic matter and form THMs. Another disinfectant being studied was chlorine dioxide, which has been used to kill bacteria in European water supplies for more than twenty-five years.

It seems that THMs can be reduced or eliminated while water is disinfected thoroughly. And methods exist to remove most organic chemicals from water without the use of chlorine. Improved treatment costs more, though, and many water companies have balked at the prospect of raising rates. Company officials and local politicians like to keep water cheap, in order to attract industry and to please consumers who have always had low rates. But by skimping on modern water treatment, people may pay dearly in the future—with their health.

Part of the problem is that many people don't know about the invisible chemicals in their drinking water. Once they are better informed, they are likely to accept higher water bills, knowing that their money is paying for safer water.

Water from Atlantic City's system was distributed to people whose private wells were poisoned by seepage from a landfill. (Photo by B. Vartan Boyajian/NYT Pictures)

4. Trouble Underfoot

In the 1970s, when the drinking water of many cities was analyzed, Tucson, Arizona, had the lowest number of chemical impurities. Since Tucson's water is pumped from underground, this seemed to confirm a common notion—that groundwater is protected from pollution because soils act as a barrier to contaminants. To the surprise of EPA chemists, however, high numbers of chemical compounds were found in the drinking water of Miami, which also relies mostly on groundwater.

All over the country there are reports of contaminated wells and of people forced to rely on bottled water or on jugs of water obtained from friends or relatives until a safe supply can be found. Wells in one New York town were fouled with toluene, xylene, and benzene. Toluene can affect the central nervous system. Xylene irritates the eyes, lungs, and intestinal tract. Benzene is a cause of leukemia. All are components of gasoline. Officials investigated several underground gasoline storage tanks but found no leaks. The source of the impurities in well water remained a mystery.

In western Pennsylvania, wells in fifteen different places over a 5,000-square-mile area were closed because traces of trichloroethylene (TCE) were found. TCE is a grease-cutting compound used in industry, in septic tank cleaners, and in

49

some commercial spot removers. Besides affecting the liver, kidneys, and central nervous system, TCE causes cancer. According to the EPA, concentrations greater than 4.5 parts per billion make water unsafe. In all of the wells closed in Pennsylvania, concentrations were higher, and in most cases, the source of the chemical was unknown. This was also true of TCE found in wells in the San Gabriel Valley, California, where, in 1980, TCE contamination caused the closing of public wells serving 400,000 people.

Tetrachloroethylene, closely related to TCE, has been found in wells in Florida, Idaho, Massachusetts, and New Jersey. In most cases, the source of the contaminant could not be found. Similarly, the origin of forty-two organic chemicals and twenty-two metals in the well water of Woburn, Massachusetts, was a mystery. The most heavily contaminated water was near industries that use a lot of water in their operations. Though industries and landfills are often prime suspects in cases like these, wastes from auto garages, dry-cleaning shops, laundries, and even private homes can contaminate groundwater. Tracing a pollutant to its source is often impossible.

Some, however, are easily traced. Near Stockton, California, a chemical company was suspected as the source of the pesticide DBCP found in well water in 1979. California had outlawed DBCP in 1977 after tests showed that workers involved in its manufacture had become sterile. Investigators obtained company memorandums that told of the company's dumping tons of DBCP into unlined waste ponds near the chemical plant. There was evidence that the pesticides were carried through the soil by water and eventually reached wells. California and federal agencies filed a $45-million damage suit against the chemical company.

So far, polluted groundwater represents only a tiny fraction of the well water used by people. The resource itself is enormous—perhaps fifty times greater than all of the water in U.S. rivers and lakes. But the discovery of impurities in groundwater has frightening implications. Groundwater has always been considered to be water of the finest quality, protected from the nasty stuff that so easily pollutes water on the surface. Now we know it can be contaminated.

Even worse, we now know that groundwater lacks some self-cleaning characteristics of rivers and lakes. Water on the surface can cleanse itself of many kinds of impurities—through dilution, the effect of sunlight, and the action of aquatic organisms. These factors are absent or minimal in groundwater. As a result, groundwater may become more polluted and stay polluted longer than surface water. In surface water, for example, the highest concentrations of TCE ever found were 160 parts per billion. But a level of over 27,000 parts per billion was found in a Pennsylvania well.

Since impurities do not disperse easily in aquifers, groundwater may be polluted in one place and perfectly safe a short distance away. Hydrologists have found that "plumes" of pollutants form and move slowly through aquifers. Costly drilling is required to detect the area of a plume and to measure its movement. Cleanup involves pumping out and treating vast amounts of water before returning it to the aquifer. This is very expensive, especially in the case of a major contamination. On Long Island, New York, for example, more than 100,000 gallons of jet fuel were spilled at an air force base. The resulting plume is moving seaward at the rate of a foot a day, polluting wells as it goes, and is considered to be too expensive to clean up.

DEPENDENT ON GROUNDWATER

Concern about contaminated groundwater is greatest where

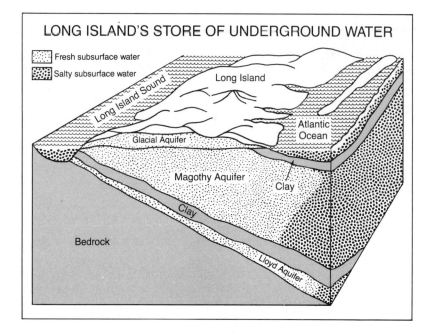

LONG ISLAND'S STORE OF UNDERGROUND WATER

people rely entirely on groundwater for all their water needs. One such place is Long Island, New York.

Long Island was formed by glaciers between 40,000 and 60,000 years ago. As ice sheets retreated northward, they deposited sand and gravel in two long ridges that today form a double spine along the length of the island. The sandiness of the soils affects what happens to the region's forty inches of annual rainfall. Water quickly soaks into the soil. There is little runoff and therefore no large rivers.

The rainfall replenishes not one but three great aquifers. The upper glacial aquifer begins right at the surface and extends to a depth of fifty to a hundred feet. A layer of clay separates this aquifer from the Magothy aquifer, which extends hundreds of feet deep. Another clay layer separates it from the deepest aquifer, the Lloyd, parts of which are more than 1,000 feet deep. Below the Lloyd aquifer is solid bedrock.

Surrounded by salt water, the huge island holds a vast store of groundwater. Even in a year of low rainfall, a storm may cause flooding in low-lying areas. Hydrologists say that it would take several years of drought to cause the water table to drop significantly. Tully Robison, a hydrologist for the U.S. Geological Survey, said, "The island has one of the best natural sources of drinking water in the country. We have a minimum 500-year supply, so long as we don't mess it up."

That possibility exists. Water supplies at the western, most densely populated end of Long Island have been thoroughly messed up. The boroughs of Brooklyn and Queens cover the land there. They were once rural or semirural suburbs of Manhattan. As these communities grew, they depleted groundwater supplies so that ocean water seeped inland. Since 1947, Brooklyn and most of Queens have relied on the New York City water system. East of Brooklyn and Queens is Nassau County, solidly suburban. Suffolk County occupies the rest of Long Island. There is great contrast between Suffolk's densely settled western end and its mostly rural end. In western Suffolk and Nassau, there is little open space left. One lure to both industrial and residential development has been easy access to "unlimited" water, just a few feet underground. Two and a half million people live in Nassau and Suffolk counties, and all of their drinking water comes from wells.

Aquifers are replenished by water only from the land surface, so what happens there affects both the quantity and quality of groundwater. Not knowing how easily aquifers could be contaminated, water managers on Long Island have for decades built catch basins to collect runoff water from streets and roads. Their goals were to keep pollutants out of the bays and coves of Long Island Sound and the Atlantic

53

Ocean, and also to maintain fresh-water pressure in the aquifers against intrusion of salt water.

Now tests of well water in mid–Nassau County show that storm water runoff is carrying chemicals from automobile emissions, industrial and commercial wastes, and household products into both the glacial and Magothy aquifers. Many wells contain traces of nitrates, probably from fertilizers used on lawns. This presents water managers with a dilemma: Aquifers must be replenished with fresh water, but each rain shower may further pollute the aquifer.

A possible solution to this problem is to capture storm runoff and clean it before returning it to aquifers. A demonstration project in Nassau County has been planned for this purpose. If it is successful, similar plants will be needed in many communities. Since 1976, tests of wells all over Long Island have produced disturbing results. In the words of an engineer for the state's Department of Environmental Conservation, the tests showed "a tremendous multitype source pollution problem, with both large and small traces of contaminants."

As of 1981, about 5 percent of the wells on Long Island had high enough concentrations of pollutants to force their closing. Most of the pollution was detected in the shallowest wells, in the upper fifty to a hundred feet. To replace the water from these wells, towns drilled deeper, through the clay barrier to the Magothy aquifer, which inevitably became fouled from the aquifer above. Despite warnings that the deepest aquifer should be left untouched as a reserve for the future, some communities have penetrated the clay deposits that formerly protected it.

The city of Long Beach, on the south shore, drilled to the last reserve of pure water because excessive pumping had allowed salt water to reach intolerable levels in the Magothy aquifer. Other towns drilled to the last aquifer because this

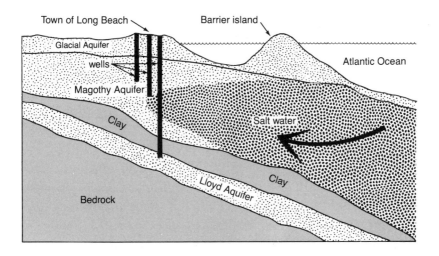

Town of Long Beach — Barrier island — Atlantic Ocean

Glacial Aquifer — wells — Magothy Aquifer — Clay — Salt water — Clay — Lloyd Aquifer — Bedrock

was the easiest, cheapest way to "solve" the problem of their polluted water supplies. But of course this just put off finding a real solution to the problem.

HOW CAN AQUIFERS BE PROTECTED?

The eastern end of Long Island was relatively free of the groundwater pollution discovered farther west. Eastern Suffolk County is mostly rural. Its farmland produces abundant crops, especially of strawberries, cauliflower, and potatoes. About 22,000 acres are usually planted with potatoes. Environmentalists and other concerned citizens have struggled to find ways to preserve Suffolk's farms, arguing that such prime lands, so close to New York City, are too precious to be used for mere housing developments. And as long as the farms survived, they believed, the aquifers beneath them would be safe from the pollution troubling other parts of the island.

But potato farmers had their own troubles: two pests named the Colorado potato beetle and the golden nematode. To combat them, in 1973, the EPA approved the use of an insecticide named Temik, a product of the Union Carbide Corporation. Temik's active ingredient is called aldicarb. If eaten by people, aldicarb causes weakness, sweating, nausea, and slurred speech. It is considered to be highly dangerous to anyone who eats food with Temik on it. For food safety, the Food and Drug Administration set an upper limit for Temik on potatoes of one part per million.

The pesticide was designed to break down quickly, usually within a week of application. In Long Island's fields, granules of Temik were spread in the soil right by the seed potatoes as they were planted. The potato plants absorbed Temik as they grew, and this made the plants poisonous to the pests. Since Temik had been used successfully elsewhere, no problems were expected on Long Island.

Unfortunately, neither the chemical company nor the EPA had taken Long Island's special geology into account. Rain quickly washed some Temik deep into the porous soils before the pesticide could break down. In 1979, traces of Temik were found in well water near potato fields. Eventually more than a thousand wells were found to be contaminated. The New York State Health Department issued a general warning against drinking water from the island's potato-farming region, and Union Carbide withdrew Temik from use on Long Island.

Officials and scientists disagreed about the health risk to people. Since Temik had not previously been found in water, no safety standards had been set. Union Carbide claimed that concentrations of 200 parts per billion were safe. The EPA tentatively set a limit of 30 parts per billion. Besides uncertainty about Temik's danger, no one knew whether the pesticide would eventually break down or persist in the aquifer.

Pest control experts searched for a new way to combat

More than a thousand wells were contaminated after the pesticide Temik was applied to Long Island potato fields.

potato pests on Long Island. There was a new urgency to find a nonchemical control method. Geologist Steven Englebright said, "Any pesticide they put down will get into the water supply. People must realize that using chemicals on the surface of Long Island is a game of high risk in which you are playing with your community's drinking water."

"Perhaps we should be glad that the Temik episode happened," said the director of a local environmental group. "It raised people's consciousness about how easily our water supply can be polluted. Maybe town officials will think harder before they make plans for garbage disposal, and householders will understand why they shouldn't throw crankcase grease from their cars and paint cans on their property."

In Florida, limestone aquifers are the main source of fresh water. The porous rock is often just a few feet beneath the surface and is easily contaminated. As a result, Florida has more hazardous waste sites than any other state, according to the EPA. And as a result of booming growth during the 1970s, Florida also has a declining water table, coastal salt water intrusion, and sharp competition for water between regions of the state and between rural and urban dwellers.

Referring to the threat of pollution to other eastern areas blessed with abundant underground water supplies, Steven Englebright said, "Around Washington, D.C., it is probably too late. But local governments in the Carolinas, Virginia, and the Gulf states can still protect their large interior spaces as watersheds. They should set aside their upland areas in large contiguous blocks, use them for recreation, and refuse to allow subdivision. It's hard for people to understand the need to protect reservoirs they can't see, but if they don't, Long Island's experience will be repeated again and again."

Not far away, powerful economic and political forces seemed bent on ignoring the lessons of Long Island. In southern New Jersey, real estate speculators and developers covet a large, mostly unsettled space called the Pine Barrens or Pinelands. It covers nearly a fourth of the state. And beneath the Pinelands lies the Cohansey aquifer—2,350 square miles of sand, gravel, and clay that hold an estimated 17 trillion gallons of water. Seldom does the aquifer lie more than twenty feet underground.

Most of the aquifer is unpolluted because most of the Pinelands is covered with forest. (Similar scrubby forest occurs in parts of eastern Long Island and is the last major untouched aquifer-recharge area there.) The Pinelands has a few small towns and blueberry and cranberry farms. The area is laced with ribbons of swamps and with small rivers that are

The Cohansey aquifer augments the flow of small rivers, but most of this huge store of water lies beneath New Jersey's Pinelands.

among the most popular canoeing streams in the Northeast. These so-called Barrens have a rich variety of plants and animals, including several endangered species of reptiles and amphibians.

Most of the Pinelands are beyond reasonable commuting distance of major cities. The soils are unsuited to most kinds of agriculture. The Pinelands escaped much development until the 1970s. Then retirement housing projects and shopping malls began spreading inland from the coast. The legalization

59

of casino gambling in Atlantic City stimulated a growth boom that spread west. The Pinelands began to disappear fast.

A coalition of environmental groups tried to save a large, unspoiled portion. Their cause would have failed, probably, if they were defending only wildlife and recreation resources. But the great water resource of the Cohansey aquifer was also at stake. Several years of intense political struggle in New Jersey and Washington produced a unique federal and state plan to protect 1.1 million acres—and the water beneath. Plans for the Pinelands National Reserve were approved in the last few days of the administration of President Jimmy Carter.

According to the plan, almost no development can occur in the central, least-developed area, and building is limited in a larger, surrounding buffer zone. This federal-state plan was hailed by land-use planners across the nation. If it works, it will undoubtedly be applied elsewhere. Whether it would be given a chance to succeed was in doubt, however. The plan's implementation depended partly on federal funds for land purchase and administration. And the Pinelands National Reserve faced a formidable array of local politicians, land speculators, builders, and other powerful interests who lobbied in New Jersey and Washington to weaken its zoning laws, reduce its operating funds, or scuttle it entirely.

Even as they tried to undo the protection plan, however, evidence mounted that the Pineland's great water resource needed that protection. In homes only five years old, people discovered that their wells had become polluted from their own septic systems. And in Jackson Township, 167 families were forced to go without tap water for nearly two years. Water from their wells—drawn from the Cohansey aquifer— had been found to contain acetone, benzene, chloroform, TCE, toluene, and other chemicals that had leached (dissolved and washed out) from a landfill. Once the chemicals were discovered, in 1977, the families relied on water trucked to their homes until a new water system, supplied from an uncontaminated part of the aquifer, was set up.

James McCarthy, a Jackson Township resident, said, "According to the Environmental Protection Agency, we are number fourteen on a list of twenty-five of the hottest toxic chemical-contaminated spots in the United States. I've been drinking polluted water for seven years."

McCarthy had a diseased kidney removed, and his young daughter died of a rare form of cancer. People tended to blame virtually any illness on water they had drunk. But there was no way to prove conclusively that polluted water had caused an unusual incidence of kidney diseases or other ailments in the community. Health experts disagreed about the extent of risk from the impurities found in the aquifer. There was no doubt, however, that people in Jackson Township would live with fear for themselves and for their children and grandchildren, because of the possibility of cancer and birth defects.

It was later discovered that their wells had drawn water from a plume of poisons, about four miles long, that began at the town landfill and moved seaward. The plume is expected to seep along at the pace of a few feet a year and may remain hazardous for centuries.

A landfill near Atlantic City, closed in 1976, yielded an underground plume of toxic chemicals that by 1981 had flowed close to wells that produced part of the city's drinking water from the Cohansey aquifer. Atlantic City rushed to find and develop a new well field. The estimated cost was $7 million, but the city had no choice—the old wells had to be abandoned.

Methods for purifying polluted aquifers are being investigated. In one system, filters of activated carbon are attached

Buried in this abandoned landfill are toxic chemicals that threaten the water supply of Atlantic City, New Jersey.

to wells and the carbon captures the pollutants. Another filtering method uses columns of resins that absorb pollutants from water. In a third method, water pumped from an aquifer and up a tower is then sprayed into the air. Many of the chemical compounds evaporate before the water hits the ground and seeps back into the aquifer.

These methods are expensive, but they will probably be needed increasingly if people continue to be careless about the waters hidden beneath their feet. The simplest way to deal with contaminated aquifers is to avoid polluting them in the first place.

Some additional steps to protect aquifers have been taken. The EPA found that local governments and industries in the United States operated 650,000 injection wells, used to pump sewage and chemical wastes underground or to force water into the earth in order to help recover oil. In 1980, the agency issued safety regulations on these injection wells. They included capping wells that discharge hazardous wastes directly into aquifers. The EPA also began to exert control over industrial settling ponds and lagoons where chemicals are stored or separated, many of which were unlined and were leaching toxic wastes into groundwater. The agency also devised a "groundwater protection strategy" to be recommended for adoption by the states.

Drawing up plans is easy, but carrying them out is another matter. To keep wastes out of aquifers calls for a degree of change and commitment that people don't often give unless they feel they are in a crisis. If they don't act until then, their water supplies may be poisoned, and their feelings of urgency and a desire to change will have come too late.

Scarcity of water has sometimes been a harsh reality in the West, and the demands on limited supplies increase each year.

5. Bottom of the Well

A traveler from the East, driving through the arid West, may notice a small but significant symbol of the contrasts between the regions. In the East, most streams and even sizable rivers have no road signs naming them—after all, they're *only* water. In the West, an easterner may be surprised to see signs naming the tiniest, trickling creeks—after all, they're *water*.

With the exception of the Pacific Northwest, the West gets less than twenty inches of rain a year. (These arid lands are generally considered to be west of the 100th meridian, an imaginary line that runs north and south, from the middle of North Dakota through the middle of Texas.) Scarcity of water has had a powerful effect on the land and its people. In the next few decades it will have an even greater effect.

About a century ago, some people believed that much of the West was destined always to be lightly settled and little used. John Wesley Powell, famed for his exploration of the Grand Canyon, prepared a report on the arid West for Congress. He emphasized the natural limits of its water resources and of the land that could be irrigated. He concluded that "these lands will maintain but a scanty population."

In 1893, Powell addressed the International Irrigation Congress in Los Angeles. A hostile audience booed his ideas about the limits set by water in the West. Powell said, "I tell you gentlemen, you are piling up a heritage of conflict and litigation over water rights, for there is not sufficient water to supply the land."

Some people believe that Powell was basically correct, and that it just took a century for his words to come true. Others say that he was wrong—then and now.

Today the arid West is booming in population growth and in agricultural and energy production. Arid lands produce 66 percent of the nation's cotton, 39 percent of its barley, and 21 percent of its wheat. Southern California alone accounts for a sizable portion of the fruit and vegetables produced in the United States. Maps of the West are dotted with active or proposed energy projects, including uranium mining, oil and natural gas drilling, and coal mining. Most of the nation's fastest growing cities are in the arid West. All this is possible because of some technological devices and feats that Powell could not foresee—huge dams, powerful pumps, highly mechanized irrigation equipment, and systems that carry water hundreds of miles, from places of relative abundance to more arid regions. It is also made possible because only a small fraction of the water's cost is paid by those who use it; the blooming of the West has been financed largely by public funds from all of the nation's taxpayers.

Much of the precipitation in the West falls as snow. So westerners became dam builders, believing that they had to catch and store water in reservoirs while it was available in the spring. State governments and private interests could not afford the billions of dollars needed for these projects. The dams have been built mostly by the Bureau of Reclamation, a federal agency created in 1902. By 1981, it had built 313 dams, 7,020 miles of irrigation diversion canals, 50 hydroelectric generators, and 134 pumping stations, at a cost of $8 billion.

Much of the water stored in the dams is used for agriculture, especially irrigated farming. But surface waters alone cannot support irrigation as it is presently practiced in the West. Enormous amounts of groundwater are also used. John Wesley Powell didn't reckon on groundwater to help irrigate crops. In his time, water was pumped by power from windmills, which produced small volumes of water rather slowly from shallow wells. Still, the precious water sustained livestock and vegetable gardens. Historian Walter Prescott wrote, "The windmill was like a flag marking the spot where a small victory had been won in the fight for water in an arid land."

Modern pumps produce more water at greater speed from greater depths. They help make most western irrigated agriculture possible. At first, irrigation ditches were dug along the edges of fields, and water from the ditches was allowed to flow in channels between rows of crops. The land had to be almost but not quite level, so that the water would flow along the rows and reach all of the plants. In the 1930s, systems of gated pipes in fields gave irrigators more control over the flow of water. Excess water could be pumped back into the system so it didn't go to waste. Stationary sprinklers were introduced during the early 1940s. Then sprinklers that rolled across fields on giant wheels were developed.

In the 1950s, a new type of mobile sprinkler was introduced—the center pivot. Instead of rolling across fields, its sprinkler arm rotates in a circle. Water comes from a well drilled in the center of the area to be irrigated and is sprayed from nozzles in the quarter-mile-long arms that reach outward from the well. A center pivot system can irrigate as much as 160 acres at a time. This sprinkler system brought a new look to farmlands, especially when seen from the air, since fields are circular instead of square or rectangular.

In center pivot irrigation, water is sprayed from a long pipe
that rotates over crops like a hand on a clock face.

All of these irrigation methods, old and new, are practiced
in various places in the West. And much of the water they use
is groundwater. Along the eastern edge of the arid West, the
groundwater comes from the Ogallala aquifer. Named after a
western tribe of the Sioux nation, this storehouse of water was
created long before any Indians or other humans lived. Between 5 million and 24 million years ago, erosion of the eastern
front of the Rocky Mountains brought sand, gravel, and other
sediments to the lowlands. Water from the plentiful rainfall of
that period saturated these deposits and was trapped between
a bottom layer of shale and a top layer of erosion-resistant
rock.

The Ogallala aquifer may be the largest underwater reserve
of fresh water on earth. It holds an estimated 2 billion acre-
feet. (An acre-foot is the amount of water needed to cover an
acre one foot deep. It equals 325,851 gallons. It has also

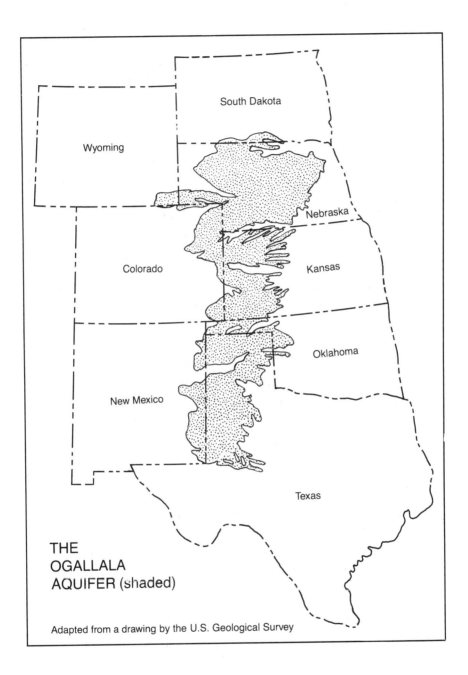

South Dakota

Wyoming

Nebraska

Colorado

Kansas

Oklahoma

New Mexico

Texas

THE
OGALLALA
AQUIFER (shaded)

Adapted from a drawing by the U.S. Geological Survey

been calculated to be enough water to fill nineteen average-sized swimming pools, or to flush 63,631 toilets, or to supply the needs of a family of five for one year.) The Ogallala stretches 800 miles, underlying parts of eight High Plains states from South Dakota to Texas. It is the main water supply for major parts of six High Plains states—Texas, New Mexico, Oklahoma, Colorado, Kansas, and Nebraska.

Most of the Ogallala's water is millions of years old and is replenished very little by the region's sparse rainfall. Water pumped from the Ogallala is not quickly replaced, as is water in Long Island's glacial aquifer or New Jersey's Cohansey aquifer. Ogallala water is more like oil pumped from underground or coal dug from the earth. In a sense, the water is being mined, and the aquifer will someday run dry. In fact, the federal government allows farmers a groundwater depletion allowance on their taxes—an acknowledgment that the resource is limited.

About 200,000 wells now puncture the High Plains. They irrigate more than 10 million acres. Ogallala water has brought a prosperous economy to the region. It enables farmers to raise corn, cotton, and other crops that could not survive if watered only by normal rainfall. The production of feed grains has led to the development of cattle feed lots, where large numbers of cattle are fattened, and to the establishment of slaughterhouses and meatpacking companies. Forty percent of all grain-fed beef sent to market in the United States is fattened in the High Plains region overlying the Ogallala aquifer.

This is an agricultural boom dependent on mined water. There is nothing inherently wrong in using up groundwater in this way, but people in the High Plains have trouble facing reality: Their wells have bottoms.

Almost all of Nebraska has access to the Ogallala aquifer. A third of the state's cultivated farmland is now irrigated, and a University of Nebraska water development expert predicted that two-thirds will be irrigated by the turn of the century. Center pivots work well on sandy soils and rolling hills where other irrigation methods fail, so the use of center pivot systems has increased rapidly and is encouraged by state agricultural officials. A former University of Nebraska president called irrigation the state's "secret weapon" and predicted that the use of irrigation and especially of center pivots could put Nebraska into the forefront of all agricultural states.

If irrigation is a weapon, then it may be a two-edged sword that will eventually puncture Nebraska's farming balloon. Conservationists and some agricultural scientists are alarmed at the effects of widespread irrigation on soils. Farmers have torn down windbreaks of trees to create bigger fields for center pivots. This invites wind erosion. Irrigation has increased erosion by water, too, and fertilizers, herbicides, and pesticides are being washed into groundwater that is tapped by wells used for drinking water.

The main source of concern in Nebraska is the leaching of nitrates, which occurs naturally in soils and also in fertilizers. Excess nitrates reduce oxygen in the blood. Infants are most vulnerable to this sometimes fatal condition, which produces a blue color in the skin and is called the blue baby syndrome. A 1978 study, based on fifty years of nitrate measurements from well water, concluded that "concentrations of nitrates in groundwater are increasing in all areas of Nebraska." The overall nitrate situation in Nebraska is not yet serious. In central Nebraska, however, intensive irrigation has brought common levels of nitrates in drinking water above the maximum concentration allowed by the EPA. This is a potentially serious health problem that is likely to worsen as irrigation continues.

More widespread is the predicament of a plummeting water

table. In parts of western Nebraska, groundwater levels have dropped as much as sixty feet. This is causing wells to run dry. In one community's wells, the water level has dropped more than twenty feet a year since 1970. And since groundwater replenishes surface water, especially in dry seasons, the flow of streams—and the fish and other life that depend on them—are threatened.

With groundwater levels dropping in many parts of Nebraska, there is concern that they may drop so low that the water will be too costly to pump. This will happen within thirty to fifty years, according to one study. In 1977, the state legislature passed a weak Groundwater Control Act. This was the first evidence of any attitude other than irrigation-boosterism by legislators. More recently, Nebraska began a four-year study of its water supply, with the aim of establishing a state water policy. Environmentalists said that the state could not afford to wait several years for more information, but should act soon to ban new irrigation wells and greater withdrawals of water from Nebraska's streams.

However, farmers are growing 130 bushels of corn an acre where they once grew 40. Irrigation has brought bountiful harvests and a level of prosperity to farmers, businesses, and towns that had never experienced anything like it. At times it seems as if they would just keep pumping until the loss of water and harm to the soil would make the land uninhabitable.

To see what the future might bring, they have only to look south, to Kansas and Texas, where groundwater mining began earlier, and where the Ogallala aquifer is thinner. Western Kansas has produced bumper corn crops since the early 1960s. Heavily irrigated land sometimes yields 152 bushels of corn an acre. By the early 1970s, however, farmers began to worry about the declining water table. Wells that used to produce 4,000 gallons a minute managed to pump only 800 gallons.

Engineering studies indicated that the water might be depleted in twenty years, and even sooner where the aquifer formation is thinnest.

No one wants the agricultural boom to end. Typically, some people are looking for a big technological solution to ensure a water supply that would allow agribusiness as usual. Diverting water from the Missouri River to western Kansas has been suggested, but the far-fetched water might cost as much as $800 an acre-foot. Other farmers are trying to stretch present supplies as best they can. Several Groundwater Management Districts have been organized. The water users who are members of these organizations set rules about spacing between wells and limits on the amount of water used.

With the help of agricultural experts, some farmers are producing good yields of corn and other grains while using half to two-thirds as much water as before. It was discovered that the season-long irrigation of corn is unnecessary. Corn plants are especially vulnerable to lack of water during their flowering-pollination period. Irrigation at that time helps ensure a good crop.

Rather than use water lavishly to achieve maximum yields, increasing numbers of farmers measure success another way —seeking the highest yield per inch of irrigation water. The aim is to use no more water than the plants need or than the soil will hold. This goal is more easily achieved in the deep loam soils of western Kansas than in the sandy soils common in much of the arid West. Loam soils store water well, whereas sandy soils do not. In western Kansas, progressive farmers are becoming skilled at measuring soil moisture and timing the use of irrigation water.

This slows the decline of the aquifer but does not stop it. A transition away from total irrigation has begun. More limited irrigation lies ahead. A return to crops that are less profitable

73

A bountiful corn crop in Nebraska, typical of the growth produced by water pumped from the Ogallala aquifer.

and that demand less water seems inevitable. Though the change may take decades, it is expected to reduce farm income, other business income, employment, land prices, and tax revenues. How soon these effects are felt and how drastic they will be remains to be seen.

FIRST TO RUN DRY

Some of these effects have already hit Texas. Around Pecos, in northwestern Texas, abandoned farmland is littered with rusting irrigation pipes. A former irrigation supply dealer described Pecos during its agricultural boom: "If ever there was a Garden of Eden, this was it. We had a thousand farmers, bumper crops of cotton and cantaloupes, fifteen cotton gins. It was *Eden*. Our water table was dropping, but manageably. Then, in 1973, natural gas prices rose too high to fuel irrigation pumps. They quit, and so did Pecos agriculture."

In the case of Pecos and some other areas of Texas, a faltering agricultural economy was balanced somewhat by a boom in oil and natural gas production. But these resources will run out, too. In the long run, the use of soil and water will determine the prosperity of the Texas High Plains. This region is part of the largest irrigable land mass in the world. The High Plains of West Texas and eastern New Mexico contain 52 million acres of fertile land that could be irrigated. For now, more than 6 million acres are under irrigation, mostly with water from 70,000 wells. A billion-dollar-plus economy depends on mining water from the Ogallala aquifer. Since the aquifer is thinner in the Texas High Plains than it is farther north, it is expected to be depleted first in Texas.

For decades, this was considered impossible. Although the U.S. Geological Survey explained in 1914 that the Ogallala was a reserve of mostly ancient water, Texans believed that they

Without irrigation, the High Plains seldom receive enough
rain to produce high yields of corn or other grains.

were tapping a huge underground river that arose in the
Rockies or the Arctic. This belief lasted well into the 1950s.
The underground river is a myth, and the Ogallala is being
used up. Already, thousands of acres of once irrigated land
have reverted to farmland that is dependent on twenty inches
of rainfall or less a year. This is an average, and the annual
amount varies widely. Dr. Anson Bertrand, dean of the College
of Agricultural Sciences at Texas Tech University in Lubbock,
said, "Without irrigation, this country will produce nothing at
all one-third of the time, marginal crops one-third of the time,
and excellent crops one-third of the time."

Overemphasis on cotton farming in Texas depletes both the ground-water supply and soil fertility.

Many farmers are conserving water. Near Lubbock, the decline of the water table slowed when farmers adopted less wasteful methods, such as better scheduling of irrigation. But farmers also continue practices that harm the land's long-term productivity. Strong winds erode the fine sand soils, creating a brown haze on the horizon. The majority of farmers know how to reduce soil erosion (by leaving crop residues or grass on fields) and how to maintain natural soil fertility (by crop rotation), but they feel they can't afford to take the necessary steps.

Many of them plant cotton year after year. Cotton earns more money than such crops as wheat, alfalfa, and sorghum

Throughout the West, government policies encourage water waste, especially by irrigators.

and is favored by price-support policies of the U.S. Department of Agriculture. But soil scientists predict that planting cotton continually will ruin the soil fertility in Texas just as it once did in southeastern United States.

Though cotton farming uses less water than other crops, groundwater levels continue to drop. Oil recovery efforts also consume water. Wells that no longer yield oil by normal pumping can be made productive if great amounts of water are injected into the deep oil-bearing rock formations. High oil prices have made this method of oil recovery lucrative. The more it is applied, the faster the Ogallala declines.

Texas has virtually no regulation of water use. Rules about spacing wells a certain distance apart were established in the High Plains, but there were no limits on water use. This is a negative incentive. If property owners did not conserve water while those around them did, the wasteful owners benefited in the short run. The water-depletion tax allowance, granted by the federal government, also encourages water waste. The more water pumped, the less tax paid by property owners.

Some farmers, businessmen, and politicians promote the idea of importing water to the High Plains. They argue that the region's grains, cotton, and other agricultural products are vital to the nation and that failure of its irrigation-based economy would have far-reaching economic effects. Though they acknowledge the need to save water, they dream that massive amounts of money from Congress will pay for the construction and operation of systems that import water.

One plan calls for bringing Mississippi River water to the Texas High Plains and beyond. About 12 million acre-feet of water would be diverted annually via a giant canal across Louisiana to Texas. In addition to having multibillion-dollar construction costs, this project would be expensive to operate, since the water would be pumped uphill. Summing up his views of the plan, Charles Bowden, author of *Killing the Hidden Waters*, wrote, "The state contemplates seeking water it does not own which it will move with money it does not have to a final destination where it cannot control water use."

Nevertheless, a big technological "fix" like this appeals to many people, especially when, as is common, public funds pay for it. Writing in the journal *Environment*, natural resources expert David Sheridan expressed concern about the cost of rescuing the agricultural economy of the Texas High Plains: "In our society, billion-dollar-plus private economic interests do not lose their investments meekly. They seek aid from the federal government, that is, the general public. When the Ogallala aquifer water runs out, the farmers, bankers, irrigation system manufacturers, fertilizer producers, and others who have built their livelihoods from the overdraft of this resource will form a powerful lobby."

There was a time when such powerful interests could easily have their way. But the cheap energy era is over, so water transfer projects are enormously costly, and likely to become more so. Also, people in water-rich areas are now more inclined to guard their resources, with an eye to future needs and growth. In other states, it is unlikely people will feel they have enough surplus water for Texas or other areas that are using up the Ogallala aquifer.

The entire aquifer and the irrigation-economy of the High Plains are the subject of several studies by federal agencies. The U.S. Geological Survey is exploring an aquifer that lies deep *beneath* the Ogallala in many places. The Dakota aquifer formed between 96 million and 138 million years ago. Preliminary information indicates that it cannot be counted on to rescue the irrigators of the High Plains. The water is stored in sandstone and is more difficult to pump than Ogallala water. Furthermore, the Dakota water is more than 1,500 feet deep and would be costly to bring to the surface. It may also be so salty that it would have to be treated before use—another energy-consuming, expensive step.

Throughout Ogallala country, from Nebraska to Texas, some people are facing the disturbing idea that John Wesley Powell may have been right. Their wells have bottoms, and when the groundwater is mostly gone, the economy that depended on its extravagant use will be gone. The best they may be able to do is to use every drop wisely and to stretch the supply as far as possible into the future.

Snowfall in mountain ranges is the major source of water in much
of the arid West.

6. Down the Colorado

The water molecules in a snowflake that falls in northern Colorado may travel to the Gulf of California, 1,450 miles away. During its journey down the Colorado River, the water will be used and returned to the river two or three times. Actually, most of the water from melted snow in Colorado never reaches the sea. It is more likely to reach the mouths of people—through lettuce, melons, strawberries, tomatoes, or other irrigated foods—than to reach the river's mouth.

The Colorado River begins in Rocky Mountain National Park, flows west out of the Rockies, then cuts south through Utah and Arizona. Such tributaries as the Green, Dirty Devil, and Little Colorado rivers add to its flow. It winds through the Grand Canyon, then south along the California border and into Mexico before reaching the sea. The Colorado drains one-twelfth of all the land in the United States, yet it is not a large river. It carries nearly 15 million acre-feet annually, somewhat more than the Delaware. The Delaware, however, is one river among many in the East. The Colorado is the only significant source of surface water in the Southwest.

Seventeen million people in seven states and part of Mexico depend on it. With fourteen major dams, it is the most controlled river system in the United States. Hydroelectric power produced at the dams helps pump water up mountains and push it to cities and farmland far from the river. The Colorado is the most fought-over river in the country. As the lifeblood of an arid and fast-growing region, its use will bring more conflict in the future.

Competition for the river's water begins within the state of Colorado. Irrigators tap the young river even before it reaches the first of several reservoirs. From these reservoirs, tunnels carry water through the mountains to the dry eastern slope of the Rockies, where it supplies such cities as Denver, Fort Collins, and Colorado Springs. It also irrigates thousands of acres of farmland. (In eastern Colorado, irrigators mine water from the Ogallala aquifer.)

People living on the western slope of the Rockies resent this diversion of water that once flowed their way. They are concerned that the booming growth of Denver will mean less water for western Colorado. Some people say that Denver will be a "new Houston"—a gloomy prospect in terms of water supplies, especially since Denver lacks water meters.

In addition to this east-west conflict, possible competition for water looms within the western Colorado region itself. Vast deposits of coal and oil shale await development there, and production of these energy sources requires water. In the case of oil shale, the estimated water demands are not great. According to the Colorado Water Conservation Board, there is enough local water in western Colorado to support an industry that would extract 1.3 million barrels of oil from shale each day.

The high-altitude irrigated agriculture of the region is rather marginal, and some farmers have been pleased to sell their water rights to energy developers. Also, some of the energy companies acquired other water rights decades ago. Waste products from oil shale processing may pose a problem, though. They contain salts and arsenic. There is uncertainty about the health risks to people, and whether significant amounts of toxic substances would leach into waters that drain into the Colorado River system.

Coal-liquefaction plants are another matter. Simply strip-mining the coal poses great pollution control problems. And one large coal-liquefaction plant would consume 12,000 acre-feet of water a year (to produce about 50,000 barrels of oil a day). Since scores of such plants are proposed, water supply is a serious issue in western Colorado and in adjoining areas that harbor the earth's largest known deposits of coal.

Other energy development ventures in the West use and often contaminate water. Eighty percent of the nation's uranium mining occurs in Wyoming and New Mexico. Mining activity brings radioactive-contaminated water and wastes (called tailings) to the surface. Radioactive elements routinely enter groundwater and water in streams. Effluents from uranium mines and mills increase the levels of radium at several points in the Colorado River system.

In 1979, a uranium tailings dam in New Mexico broke and sent 100 million gallons of radioactive liquid down the Rio Puerco River. The contaminants reached the Little Colorado River, then the Colorado River and Lake Mead, the source of some of southern California's drinking water. By then the radioactive elements were much diluted, and it was difficult to say whether they represented a health risk to people. Close to the site of the accident, dangerous levels of radioactivity were measured in groundwater, and some wells were closed.

DIVIDING IMAGINARY WATER SUPPLIES

Although most of the Colorado River's water comes from

Competition for water in the Colorado Basin will increase as
oil shale and coal-liquefaction plants begin operating.

melting snow in Colorado, Wyoming, Utah, and New Mexico,
these Upper Basin states get to use less than half of its flow.
A division of the Colorado's water was arranged in 1922, signed
by the seven participating states, and later amended to allow
Mexico a share. The Colorado River Compact gives first rights
to the end of the line and last rights to the place of origin.
Mexico can claim 1.5 million acre-feet. States of the Lower
Basin—Arizona, Nevada, and California—get the next 7.5
million acre-feet. The four Upper Basin states are also entitled
to 7.5 million acre-feet.

Thus a total of 16.5 million acre-feet is allotted by the compact. Unfortunately, the river hasn't carried that much water in decades. The shares set by the compact were based on studies conducted before 1922, during an unusually wet period in the river's history. The Colorado rarely carries more than 14.8 million acre-feet. Thus about 120 percent of its flow is committed. Fortunately, neither the Lower nor the Upper Basin uses its full allotment yet, so the river is about 85 percent used.

As water needs increase in Colorado and other Upper Basin states, the Colorado River Compact seems more and more inequitable to residents of these states. In dry years, especially, people in Colorado resent the idea that Californians may be washing cars, using hoses to clear fallen leaves from sidewalks and driveways, and filling swimming pools with water that came from the Rocky Mountains. However, courts have upheld the legality of the Colorado River Compact, though disputes between states have led to some court-ordered adjustments.

In 1963, the U.S. Supreme Court allowed Arizona more water than before. It set California's share at 4.4 million acre-feet and Arizona's at 2.8 million acre-feet. This helped launch the Central Arizona Project, which was dreamed about for decades and authorized by Congress in 1968. It is a system of aqueducts, tunnels, and pumps that will bring an average of 1.2 million acre-feet of Colorado River water 300 miles to central and southern Arizona (including Phoenix and Tucson). Completion of this project in the mid-1980s will almost certainly overtax the river's flow. California will be the big loser, since it has been allowed to take about a million extra acre-feet until the Central Arizona Project is completed.

The Central Arizona Project is designed to fill about two-thirds of a huge groundwater overdraft in Arizona. Aquifers

Seven southwestern states and Mexico are legally entitled to more water than is usually carried by the Colorado River.

supply 62 percent of all water consumed in Arizona. (In general, aquifers west of the Ogallala are smaller and fewer in number than those in the East, and the water in them tends to be more heavily laden with salts and minerals.) As in other western states, the main use of groundwater—nearly 90 percent—is irrigation. In addition, the city of Tucson depends entirely on groundwater. It is the largest city in the United States to do so.

Throughout Arizona, groundwater is being used twice as fast as it is being replenished. In Tucson, the rate is five times as fast. Until the 1930s, the Santa Cruz River flowed through town. Now its channel is dry; it is a river of sand and gravel. Water levels in some Tucson wells have dropped 110 feet in ten years.

The sinking of land—called subsidence—in and near Tucson was predicted to begin in 1985. It occurs because water occupies space underground. When formations of soils and rocks are drained of water, they sink in irregular and unpredictable ways. This subsidence also has a long-term consequence: Once an aquifer compresses from lack of water, it loses forever some of its water-storing capacity.

Groundwater pumping has caused some spectacular subsidence between Tucson and Phoenix. According to the U.S. Geological Survey, 120 square miles of land southeast of Phoenix have sunk more than seven feet since 1952. Groundwater pumping caused a ten-mile-long ridge to form along a geological fault. Great cracks have formed, many more than a thousand feet long and ten feet deep. Some are sixty feet deep. They have damaged highways, railroad tracks, irrigation canals, and homes. In Tucson, the predicted subsidence will cause much more damage as it affects building foundations, utility lines, and even water pipes. (In Houston, Texas, excessive groundwater use causes an annual loss of $32 million in repairs and property value losses; land sinking also makes the city highly vulnerable to a surge of ocean water pushed inland by a hurricane. Subsidence caused by groundwater mining has also damaged structures in southern California and in Miami, Florida.)

Declining water tables forced some Arizona farmers to give up, as they could no longer afford to pump water to the surface. More than 50,000 acres of formerly irrigated land have been abandoned. By 1981, the city of Tucson had bought about 12,000 acres of surrounding farmland in order to obtain the water rights. City officials hoped to buy an additional 36,000 acres by 1985. This would just about finish irrigated farming (of cotton and pecans) in the Tucson area.

Tucson residents were urged to save water, but this was a

Groundwater pumping has caused land to sink, and to crack like
this, in the region between Phoenix and Tucson.

difficult adjustment for those who had once lived in the East
or Midwest. To these people, a home without a lawn seemed
incomplete. For them, trees, green lawns, and heavily watered
golf courses helped disguise the reality that Tucson is a desert,
receiving only eleven inches of rain a year.

In 1977, Tucson's City Council voted to raise water rates,
to encourage conservation. The much higher rates became
effective in June, a tactical error since summer is the season
of greatest water use. The shock of higher water bills caused
a political backlash and recall of the council members who
had supported the increased rates. Nevertheless, the rates
were not lowered, and many people in Tucson have since
reduced water use, in some cases by replacing lawns with

native desert plants. Between 1977 and 1980, the average daily use fell from 200 gallons to 140 gallons. This is laudatory and will help stretch groundwater supplies in the Tucson area. There are new uncertainties about the supply, though. Some of Tucson's wells are located on the edge of a Papago Indian reservation. The Papagos have sued the city, claiming that water withdrawals by Tucson have caused some reservation wells to dry up. They seek to restrain all groundwater pumping that affects water supplies on the reservation.

Residents and businesses of central Arizona look forward to the completion of the Central Arizona Project and to dependable water supplies from the Colorado River. The project is a classic example of a familiar pattern in the arid West: A regional economy is built and thrives on mined groundwater; then, when it becomes clear that the water will not last, an expensive import project is planned. In this case, the project will be completed at a cost of approximately $2.2 billion. Operating costs will be high, since water from the Colorado must be pumped up 2,000 feet in elevation. According to a 1978 study, the fifty-year cost to U.S. taxpayers will be $5.4 billion.

Water from the Central Arizona Project will be no panacea for the state's water problems. Assuming Arizona gets the water it is allotted, it will continue to mine groundwater, though at a slower pace. Also, Arizona's allotment of 1.2 million acre-feet is a fifty-year *average*. The actual amount is expected to be somewhat greater at the start of that period and to become progressively smaller. At any time, a prolonged drought, increased withdrawals by other states, or a combination of both could cut the water available to Arizona.

If water supplies were reduced, who should be given priority when allocating the remainder? City dwellers, who still waste many gallons a day? Arizona's copper mining and refining

Through pamphlets like these and awards for desert landscaping
(rather than lawns), Tucson encouraged water conservation.

industry, which supplies a quarter of the nation's copper and
also uses over 50,000 acre-feet of water annually? Or agricultural interests, which grow abundant crops of cotton, alfalfa,
citrus fruits, and wheat, yet account for only 10 percent of the
state's economy? To most observers, agribusiness is the main
cause of the area's water plight, and concern about water
supplies will ease only when irrigators adopt less wasteful ways.

Aside from an ineffective 1948 law, the state of Arizona did
little until recently to manage groundwater. Legally, if people
owned land there, they also owned as much water as they

could pump from it. Groundwater was treated as a property right rather than a public resource. (This is also true of water laws in other western states.) As the water table dropped, the conflict over water increased, but it seemed unlikely that competing interests would ever work out a way to share and save water. Then, in 1979, Secretary of the Interior Cecil Andrus threatened to delay the construction of the Central Arizona Project unless action was taken to conserve groundwater.

This stimulated intense negotiations between the main competing interests—agriculture, cities, and mining—and produced a 176-page bill that was passed by the Arizona legislature and signed into law by Governor Bruce Babbitt in 1980. The governor said, "We're going overnight from a laissez-faire system, a system where everybody used whatever they wanted wherever they wanted, to the most comprehensive groundwater management system of any state in the American West."

A goal of the law was to reduce groundwater use by the year 2225 to the "safe yield" point, at which the amount withdrawn equals the amount replaced by rainfall. Some hydrologists and environmentalists scoffed at this goal, believing that the safe yield would inevitably be reached much sooner because aquifers would be totally depleted. Nevertheless, the law brought sweeping reforms to groundwater use in Arizona. Regulations were to be put into effect over a five-year period. They included registration of all wells and prohibition of new irrigated farming in groundwater problem areas. Existing farms were required to conserve water and to pay a pump tax. A newly established Department of Water Resources had the power to buy and retire water rights of existing farms after the year 2006. Its aim was to systematically take agricultural land out of production.

The most comprehensive water management was aimed at Arizona's largest cities and its main agricultural region. The Department of Water Resources was empowered to set water consumption limits for cities. But the state's agricultural industry would feel the greatest impact of the law. Arizona had decided to cut back on farming so that cities and industries could grow.

Arizona had finally tackled a problem that most other western states had virtually ignored. Several years must pass before the effects of the new law become apparent. "But by passing such a law," wrote David Sheridan in *Environment*, "Arizona has acknowledged that groundwater is a finite resource and should be managed accordingly. This realization alone is historic."

SALT, WILDLIFE, AND WATER LAWS

When the Colorado River reaches the Morelos Dam near the Mexican border, most of its water has been used more than once for irrigation, then drained back into the river channel. Water stored by the dam is diverted into Mexican farmland, so the last flow of the river, into the Gulf of California, is mostly drainage water from those fields.

A long way from Rocky Mountain snowfields, the water has deteriorated a lot in quality. It may lack the industrial impurities common to eastern rivers, but it has gained plenty of salt. All rivers absorb salts and other minerals from the rocks and soils of their valleys. Stored in reservoirs and transported in canals, the water is reduced in volume by evaporation. Great amounts of water are lost to evaporation from reservoirs in the Lower Colorado Basin. The remaining water becomes more saline. In irrigated fields, the water picks up more salt. Drained back into the river, subjected to further evaporation, and spread onto fields again, the water becomes increasingly salty.

In the early 1960s, as a result of drainage from new irrigation east of Yuma, Arizona, salt concentrations in the Lower Colorado River reached about 1,500 parts per million—too salty for use on most crops. This was nearly double the amount of salt in water pumped to California's Imperial Valley. Used for irrigation in Mexico, the water ruined vegetable crops. Some remedial measures taken by the United States were not effective enough, so in 1973, the federal government agreed that Mexico's allotment from the Colorado will contain only about 800 parts per million of salt. To accomplish this, a desalting plant, costing up to $350 million, was built near Yuma by the Bureau of Reclamation.

Scheduled to be completed in the mid-1980s, this desalting plant was the largest of its kind. Taking salty drainage water from Arizona, each year it will produce a stream of 73,000 acre-feet of water that has only 235 parts per million of salt. The extracted salt will be carried as brine in a drain to the Gulf of California. The desalted water will be mixed with untreated drainage water so that Mexico will get its share of low-salinity water. Meeting this obligation to Mexico will cost U.S. taxpayers $250 for each acre-foot produced by the desalting plant. A much cheaper solution would have been to buy out the farmers in the irrigation district that was the main cause of excessive salt in Mexico's share of the Colorado. But a reasonable and economic remedy like this faced fierce opposition from the farmers, who did not want to sell and vowed to fight any such effort in court.

Concern about having enough water in the West for farming, industry, and cities sometimes overshadows the fact that rivers are more than conduits or storage places for water. They are also recreation places and homes for wildlife—both in the

At this site near Yuma, Arizona, desalting methods were tested
for use in the world's largest desalinization plant.

water and in the special habitats that exist along river edges
and in river valleys.

Though the Colorado River flows through wild scenery, it is
a tamed river. Most of the Lower Colorado is a series of long
pools behind dams. Reservoirs have eliminated most of the
habitat of native fishes, including the endangered Colorado
squawfish, a member of the minnow family that can grow to
be six feet long. According to fisheries experts, the ideal flow
for a fish habitat in the Lower Colorado would be 6,864 million
gallons a day; the average flow is 1,650 million gallons.

Management of the Colorado's flow also affects recreation. As a result of drought in 1977, the amount of water allowed to flow from the Glen Canyon Dam through Grand Canyon National Park was reduced. Rafts carrying tourists through the canyon were stranded, and some people had to be lifted out by helicopter. Finally, more water was released in order to flush raftloads of tourists down the river.

In most western states, water laws do not provide for the protection of fish and wildlife or recreation. Water is considered a property right, and people can lease, sell, or trade the water rights they own. They have no responsibility to keep streams flowing, as people do under water laws common in the East. They are, however, obliged to put their water to "beneficial use" at least once in several years. Otherwise, they may lose their water rights.

Beneficial uses include agriculture, private or community water supplies, and industry. They also include water for wildlife or recreation, but a quirk in the law affects *how* the water may be used for these purposes. Courts have ruled that water must actually be taken from the stream in order to qualify as a beneficial use. Diverting water to a pond where fish live is considered a beneficial use; leaving water in a river where fish live is not.

This anachronism of western water laws worries environmentalists. Although groundwater mining and increased use of surface water are causing stream flows to drop, reducing recreation opportunities for people and habitats for fish and wildlife, few western states have taken steps to reserve stream flows for these purposes. One exception is Montana, which in 1973 began to allocate rights to the water of the Yellowstone River and its tributaries. The 671-mile Yellowstone is the longest free-flowing river left in the United States outside of Alaska. Its upper portion is one of the finest trout streams in

Low flow of water in the Colorado sometimes halts recreational
use of the river.

the world. But the river's annual flow of 8.8 million acre-feet
is eyed hungrily by energy companies that hope to develop
vast coal deposits in eastern Montana. Such corporations as
Exxon, Gulf, Mobil, and Tenneco, Inc., own much of the 50
billion tons of strippable coal there. Converting this coal to
synthetic fuels would consume huge amounts of water.

In 1978, however, the Montana Board of Natural Resources
and Conservation ordered that 5.5 million acre-feet of the
Yellowstone's annual flow be reserved for the sake of water
quality and habitats for fish and wildlife. Montana's acknowledgment of these values set an important example in the
West. But fishermen, environmentalists, and others who like
the Yellowstone as it is, worry about growing pressure to
change the allocation of its water.

In addition to energy companies, Indians may affect the Yellowstone's future. South of the river lie the Crow and Northern Cheyenne reservations. The Bighorn River flows through the Crow Reservation and contributes 2.5 million acre-feet to the Yellowstone; Rosebud Creek and the Tongue River flow through the Northern Cheyenne Reservation and are also tributaries of the Yellowstone. These Indians believe they have a firm claim to the water of these rivers. A 1908 Supreme Court decision guaranteed to Indians the beneficial use of water that is adjacent to, or rises on, or flows through their reservations. If the Crow and the Northern Cheyenne use large amounts of water for agriculture or energy development, the Yellowstone's flow will be reduced. Competition for the remaining flow will intensify.

The division of water in other states is also uncertain because of Indian claims. For instance, the Colorado River Compact allots Utah 23 percent of the river water available to the Upper Basin states. But the Green River, a major tributary of the Colorado, flows along the edge of the Uinta-Ouray Reservation. Ute Indians may be entitled to much of the Green River's flow and thereby could take a significant part of Utah's water allotment.

In general, Indians in the West have not exploited the groundwater beneath their lands nor fought for a share of surface waters. But the legal and political advancement of Indian rights has focused attention on water. Along the Colorado, Indians believe that they have an original claim to the water. Twelve small tribes in Arizona claimed a portion of the water from the Central Arizona Project. They were tentatively assigned about 25,000 acre-feet in 1976 but sought a larger allotment. In 1980, then–Secretary of the Interior Andrus signed contracts with the Indians that would increase their long-range share and would also protect their water

Rivers are more than water supplies for people. The Upper Yellowstone is considered to be one of the world's finest trout streams.

rights during drought. Andrus said, "Arizona Indian tribes have been economically depressed for generations. Water from the Central Arizona Project may be their last chance to have an economic base comparable with their non-Indian neighbors."

The state of Arizona sought in court to have the contracts declared invalid—one step in what might be a long legal battle. How much water Indians are entitled to is a question that may take years to answer, but there is little doubt that they are entitled to some, and that will increase competition for water in the West.

The people who depend on the Colorado River have been living on borrowed time, and some have been living on borrowed water. Large-scale irrigation in California has been possible in part because Arizona and the Upper Basin states

100

have not exercised all of their allotted water rights. This situation will end upon completion of the Central Arizona Project and development of fossil fuels in the Upper Basin states. Seven states and Mexico will then be "entitled" to more water than the Colorado carries.

Harris Sherman, director of Colorado's Department of Natural Resources, said, "There are going to be some very crucial direct confrontations between agriculture, municipalities, and energy industries, and there's going to be fierce competition between the states." His words echoed John Wesley Powell's 1893 warning about "piling up a heritage of conflict and litigation over water rights."

Predictably, some of those dependent on the Colorado River see a way out of their dependency—reaching outside their river basin for more water. One plan called for tapping the Snake River in Idaho, about 600 miles from Lake Mead on the Colorado. Another called for bringing water from the Columbia River, through Oregon to California, and then to Lake Mead. Both projects would require expensive over-mountain pumping. Both were vigorously opposed by people in the Northwest.

The Columbia is the fourth largest river in North America. Every day it discharges into the Pacific four times as much water as the entire state of California uses. Its flow is more than ten times that of the Colorado. Yet, in a different way, it is also overextended and a source of growing competition within its own basin. The Columbia and its tributaries contain about one-third of the nation's entire hydroelectric potential. Generating plants at more than thirty dams capture most of this energy. The electricity is cheap, and people in the Northwest have had decades of practice as energy wastrels. Until the late 1970s, they used electricity at twice the per-capita national average.

101

People in the Columbia River Basin are unlikely to agree to
diversion of water to the Southwest (Union Pacific Railroad Photo).

Then drought reduced hydroelectric power, and north-
westerners belatedly began to end their wasteful ways. They
want to attract more industry and are fearful of electrical
blackouts, however, so they don't want to lose a single gallon
of water that can produce electricity as it flows downstream.
Conflicting uses in the river basin already reduce hydroelectric potential at times. Increasing amounts of water are
withdrawn for irrigation. Indians and the fishing industry are
fighting for the remnants of the river's salmon fishery. Federal

102

courts have ruled that a flow adequate to preserve Indian fishing rights must be maintained. As competition for Columbia River water intensifies, no one is inclined to send any to the Southwest.

In fact, opposition to this idea was so strong that the bill which authorized the Central Arizona Project in 1968 won congressional approval only after it was amended to forbid for ten years any study of water importation to the Colorado River system. A Washington observer said, "When the Congress tells you that you can't even *study* something, then you know there's a real political problem."

Nevertheless, plans to bring water from the Northwest to the Southwest were later revived. The attitude that supports such plans was interpreted by a University of Arizona hydrologist: "It's the type of solution Americans like. It relieves them of individual responsibility to live within the limitations of their resources."

7. California Pipe Dream

The idea of moving huge amounts of water hundreds of miles is old stuff to Californians. Los Angeles exhausted its own limited water supplies around 1900 and began reaching north. Today, 70 percent of water use is in southern California, while 70 percent of the state's natural water supply is in the north. So California has one of the world's largest systems of dams, pumping plants, tunnels, and aqueducts. Moving all the water takes 4 billion kilowatt-hours of electricity, making the state's water projects the single largest consumer of electricity. California has about two hundred major reservoirs, including six with a capacity of a million acre-feet or more. Only a few rivers have been left undammed.

California's water once flowed from east to west. Now most of it flows from north to south. Reservoirs in the Sierras and the Trinity Mountains, in north-central California, send water via canals into the Central Valley, where major irrigation begins. Water in the state's main canal, the California Aque-

The California Aqueduct carries water more than four hundred miles from a northern reservoir to Central Valley farmlands.

duct, is pumped 2,000 feet over the Tehachapi Mountains to Los Angeles. The Imperial Valley, which begins about 120 miles southeast of Los Angeles, is supplied with Colorado River water pumped north through the All-American and Coachella canals. San Diego obtains Colorado River water via another aqueduct, while Los Angeles and San Francisco fill part of their water needs with their own reservoirs in the Sierras. Finally, more than a third of the state's water comes from aquifers.

Only 15 percent of California's water is used for drinking and bathing by people, or by industry. Irrigated agriculture takes 85 percent. The Central Valley was developed first. The valley is flat and highly fertile, stretching 450 miles long and 30 to 60 miles wide. The smaller Imperial Valley, just north of Mexico, also has deep, rich soil and a long growing season. It is the single biggest consumer of Colorado River water, taking 2.9 million acre-feet a year. In southern California, rain is often considered a nuisance, something that interferes with the schedule for applying irrigation water.

All together, 9 million acres are irrigated in California—a fifth of all irrigated farmland in the nation. This land produces about 40 percent of the country's fresh fruit and vegetables, valued at $9.2 billion in 1980. By itself, the San Joaquin Valley, which is the southern half of the Central Valley, outproduced all but three states—Iowa, Texas, and Illinois—in farm products.

California irrigation means thriving agribusiness, jobs for long-haul truckers, tax revenues for the state and federal governments, cotton for clothes, rice exported to Japan, and food for people from Los Angeles to Maine. Cheap water helps make all this possible. And the irrigation water is cheap because most of the construction, pumping, and maintenance costs of the water projects are paid for by the general public. Some

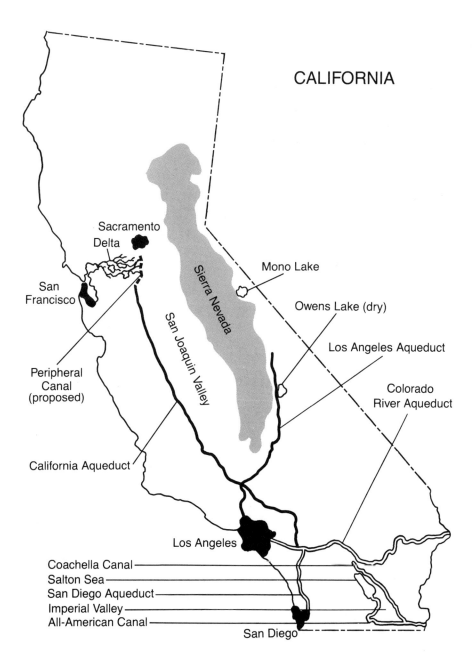

CALIFORNIA PIPE DREAM

CALIFORNIA

Sacramento
Delta
Mono Lake
San
Francisco
Owens Lake (dry)
Los Angeles Aqueduct
Peripheral
Canal
(proposed)
Colorado
River Aqueduct
California Aqueduct
Los Angeles
Coachella Canal
Salton Sea
San Diego Aqueduct
Imperial Valley
All-American Canal
San Diego

Sierra Nevada

San Joaquin Valley

Machines harvest radishes in California. The plants were irrigated with Colorado River water, carried by the Coachella Canal.

people wonder whether this is a sound bargain. They also wonder whether California agribusiness, and that of other arid states, can or should continue to operate as it has.

The period 1976–1977 was the driest on record in California, yet the state suffered only about a $500 million loss in agricultural income. This was accomplished because California was able to take 5.6 million acre-feet of water from the Colorado River in 1977. Upon completion of the Central Arizona Project, California will be limited to 4.4 million acre-feet. California has been aware of this situation for years and has taken steps or made plans to get more water. One long overdue step was to line the Coachella Canal with concrete, thus saving an estimated 132,000 acre-feet of Colorado River water that used to seep into the desert each year.

This water-conserving step was hailed by environmentalists,

East of San Francisco, the Sacramento and San Joaquin rivers
join in the Delta, a region of rich farmland.

who believe that more emphasis must be put on ways to save
water, not on finding and moving more. But the state and
federal governments continued to pursue expensive, energy-
consuming, structural solutions—canals, reservoirs, and pumping facilities. The most expensive proposal is called the
Peripheral Canal. It was designed to move even more water
from the state's northern rivers to the arid south. It was also
supposed to help solve complicated water problems in the
Delta, a 1,100-square-mile area east of San Francisco, where
the Sacramento and San Joaquin rivers meet to form the headwaters of San Francisco Bay. The Delta is a maze of waterways,
small islands, and farmlands protected by dikes. It is highly
productive in both farming and commercial fishing.

109

A lush growth of shrubs in the desert revealed where water once leaked from California's Coachella Canal.

River water from the Delta area is pumped south by both the state and federal governments, and the state hoped to withdraw twice as much as before. But this would reduce the local water supply, let salt water intrude into farmland, and cut the amount of fresh water flowing into San Francisco Bay, to the detriment of fish and other aquatic life. These effects would be avoided, according to the Peripheral Canal plan, by building new reservoirs on the Sacramento River that would

Lining the canal with concrete stopped such leaks, and saved
an estimated 132,000 acre-feet of water each year.

increase the flow of fresh water to the Delta, particularly during high tides. The Peripheral Canal itself would take much of the flow of the Sacramento River before it reached the Delta and carry it south to the California Aqueduct. This would be no simple engineering feat, because the water would have to be siphoned *under* three rivers and several other waterways.

This plan had plenty of critics, one of whom called it "a political, financial, and engineering nightmare." Many people in the San Francisco Bay area feared that the project would fail to ensure adequate fresh water for the Delta. Northern Californians in general resented sending more water south, especially after their experience in the drought of 1976–1977, when they reduced their water use by 30 to 40 percent while Los Angeles residents had an abundance of water, most of it imported from the north. (During the drought, Los Angeles refused to set any mandatory water-saving measures until forced to by a court decision.) Many economists and hydrologists believed that the Peripheral Canal project was unnecessary and uneconomic. Instead of getting more water for irrigators, they contended, the state should force them to use water sparingly.

Opponents also asserted that the project would benefit only a few large landowners. Though some farms are family-owned and -operated, most irrigated land in California is controlled by such corporations as Tenneco, Inc., Union Oil, Getty Oil, Shell Oil, Standard Oil of California, and the Southern Pacific Railroad. A 1978 study in Kern County, north of Los Angeles, showed that 85 percent of all irrigation water was used by fifteen large corporations. Consumer and environmental groups argued that giving more tax-subsidized water to such landowners was "socialism for the rich."

Those who are accustomed to being supplied with cheap

water aren't about to lose an opportunity for more. California agribusiness has a lot of political power. In 1980, the state legislature authorized the Peripheral Canal project. Soon afterward, almost a million residents signed a petition seeking a repeal referendum, to be held in 1982. Even if the repeal failed, there was doubt about whether the project would ever be built.

NORTH FOR MORE WATER

Another attempt to bring northern California water south also ran into difficulties. Since the early 1900s, Los Angeles has obtained most of its water from the Owens Valley, which lies 225 miles north of the city on the eastern edge of the Sierra Nevada. At that time, landowners were deceived, believing that they were aiding the development of their own irrigation system, as the city bought nearly 500 square miles in order to get the water rights. The city then built an aqueduct to carry water south. Some Owens Valley residents expressed their feelings with guns and dynamite. Resentment has never died.

In the 1940s, the Los Angeles Department of Water and Power (LADWP) extended its aqueduct 105 miles farther north, into the Mono Basin, having obtained water rights to several streams that fed Mono Lake (which lies northeast of Yosemite National Park). A second aqueduct was completed in 1970, enabling twice as much water to be carried south. Groundwater pumping began in the Owens Valley. Springs, marshes, and streams dried up. Plants that depended on near-surface water died. Valley dust storms became more frequent and began to harm surrounding forests.

Inyo County, which includes the Owens Valley, filed a lawsuit demanding an end to pumping, pending the preparation of an environmental impact statement. The legal staff of LADWP has succeeded in stalling and sidetracking the resolution of this matter for years.

In 1980, Inyo County voters approved a referendum calling for the creation of a local groundwater control commission. The LADWP called the commission illegal and claimed that the county was trying to confiscate the city's rights to Owens Valley water. This dispute also seems to be headed for years of litigation. Meanwhile, groundwater levels in the Owens Valley are sinking deeper, and farther north, Mono Lake is gradually drying up.

In the minds of most people, mountain lakes are supposed to have fine drinking water and great trout fishing. Mono Lake has neither, but it is extraordinary in other ways. It has existed for 700,000 years, fed by streams that carry melted snow down from the mountains. The lake has no outlet, so water evaporating during its long life has left high concentrations of chlorides, sulfates, and carbonates. No fish survive there. Algae, brine shrimp, and brine flies are the main forms of life. They attract great numbers of migratory birds— grebes, phalaropes, plovers—and the lake is a nesting area for nearly all of the state's population of one species of gull.

During spring and summer, the abundant brine flies and shrimp are fed upon by at least a million birds, including 100,000 Wilson's phalaropes bound for Argentina. Mono Lake is an extraordinary-looking place, too, with deposits of calcium carbonate rising out of the water like cave stalagmites. Many people feel that Mono Lake is well worth saving.

Since Los Angeles began taking water from the lake's inlet streams, its water level has dropped forty-four feet. If this continues, at some point the water will become too salty for the brine shrimp and other life in it. An Oregon State University biologist predicted that this will occur in twenty to twenty-five years if the present rate of water loss continues. When life in the water ends, the birds will die or go elsewhere. But there is no "elsewhere" like Mono Lake.

Citizens' groups and environmental organizations have tried to stop the lake's decline. They filed a suit against the LADWP, which then exhibited its practiced skill at delaying court action. In 1978, the California Department of Water Resources appointed a task force to recommend a plan to protect the natural resources of the Mono Basin. In 1979, the task force urged that Los Angeles cut its use of the basin's water by 85 percent to allow the lake's level to recover. It recommended water conservation and the reclaiming of used water in Los Angeles to make up for the loss of the basin's water. LADWP disagreed with these findings. A department spokesman emphasized an economic reason for continuing to pump the same amount of water out of the Mono Basin. Flowing downhill toward Los Angeles, the water produces hydroelectric power —a benefit that would be lost if people conserved so much water in Los Angeles that withdrawals from the Mono Basin could be stopped. The LADWP spokesman also doubted that water conservation in Los Angeles would be sufficient. "In a time of plenty," he said, "it's hard to get people to conserve."

People who care about Mono Lake or who live in the Owens Valley resent that water from the land around them and under them is piped 300 miles in order to give Los Angeles residents the sense that they live in "a time of plenty." Environmental groups are trying to persuade Californians, especially those in Los Angeles, that Mono Lake is worth saving and can be saved if everyone uses a little less water. But many southern Californians continued to think more in terms of finding new water supplies.

In 1978, the Los Angeles County Board of Supervisors formally called upon the U.S. Department of the Interior to develop a plan for diverting some of the Columbia River to the Southwest. Surprisingly, a major state agency, the Colorado River Board, responded by opposing any study of importing Columbia River water. Among the reasons listed for its position was the high cost of construction and of energy to run such a project. The board also pointed out that "agriculture, the principal water user in the Colorado River Basin, could not repay even a small portion of the cost."

SUBSIDENCE AND SALT

Some irrigators in southern California are concerned not just about future water supplies, but also about the side effects of intensive irrigation itself. Land is sinking in the San Joaquin Valley. Like the Texas High Plains and Central Arizona, the valley's agricultural prosperity depends in part on groundwater mining. Forty percent of the valley's irrigation water is pumped from aquifers. An area the size of Connecticut has subsided more than a foot, and as much as thirty feet in some places. Subsidence, and the structural damage it causes, are likely to continue because there are no regulations on the amount a property owner can pump.

The geology of the San Joaquin Valley (and of the Imperial Valley) creates a situation that also threatens its long-term productivity. Under part of the land, an impermeable layer blocks water from moving deeper. This causes a "perched" water table. It is especially troublesome because irrigation water, somewhat salty when applied to fields, becomes more saline in the soil. Because the water table is close to the surface, salty water may reach the roots of a crop. It inhibits the plants' ability to absorb water and oxygen. The plants grow poorly. In extreme cases, they die. If salty water reaches the surface, the salt is left as the water evaporates. Eventually a salt crust may form that keeps water from seeping easily into the soil.

About 400,000 acres of the San Joaquin are affected by high, salty water tables. So far, only a few fields have become too salt-encrusted for crops. Some farmers have gained a few years by planting shallow-rooted, salt-tolerant crops. According to a Bureau of Reclamation study, during the next century more than a million acres will become unproductive unless something is done. The remedy is to drain off excess groundwater. About 40 percent of San Joaquin farms have drainage systems. In some cases, wells or deep ditches are dug along the edges of fields so that excess irrigation water can be drained below the natural impermeable layer. This "solution" may cause another problem—allowing salty water to reach aquifers that are being used for irrigation.

Another method is to lay perforated pipes six to ten feet beneath the soil surface. The pipes are arranged so that unused irrigation water drains into and through them to a collecting pond. Then the water is pumped to a drain that carries it to a place where salty water will not contaminate soil or groundwater. In the Imperial Valley, irrigation drainage water is carried to the Salton Sea—the largest body of water in California. In the San Joaquin Valley, the natural sink for salty water would be the Pacific Ocean, but there are political, economic, and environmental problems in sending the valley's drainage water there.

The Bureau of Reclamation has completed eighty-two miles of a master drain to carry salty drainage water out of the San Joaquin Valley. The drain runs parallel to the San Joaquin River and discharges into a reservoir, from which the saline water gradually seeps into the river and is carried into the Delta region. Extension of this concrete-lined ditch all the way to the Delta, a total of 290 miles, has been proposed. By the year 2005, the drain would serve 500,000 acres and would have the capacity to carry off more than 3 million tons of salt annually. It would cost more than $1.2 billion in state and federal funds to build the drain. Pumping costs would be low because the water would flow downhill, beside the river.

Many questions have been raised about this project. There is growing resistance to having the general public bail out private businesses for their use and misuse of water. Consumer groups have argued that the farmers who benefit from a drainage project should pay for all or most of it.

If the master drain is built, it would carry as much as 250,000 acre-feet of salty water into the Delta. People wonder about its effect on aquatic life, drinking water, and agriculture there. The harm could be great, so alternatives are being explored. One is to pump drainage water west, over the Coast Range, to the Pacific. This is an expensive solution, both in building and operating costs. A tunnel through the mountains would also be expensive, though less costly to operate.

Desalinization plants have been proposed. An advantage is that drainage water would stay in the valley and could be used for irrigation after the salt had been removed. But desalting plants consume great amounts of energy. The water produced would cost up to $300 an acre-foot. Brine waste disposal would be an additional problem and expense. Another local solution is to build evaporation ponds. They would be lined to prevent drainage water from seeping out. The main problem with this approach is the huge volume of salty drainage water that is produced. Eventually, the highly saline ponds themselves would occupy thousands of acres on the valley floor—another Salton Sea in the making.

Every solution to the salty drainage problem has drawbacks. So far, little attention has been paid to the least costly solution —using less irrigation water. There are ways to greatly reduce water use and still maintain high crop yields. (They are described in the next chapter.) And the less water unused by plants, the less drainage water to dispose of. The problem could probably be managed locally, with evaporation ponds, instead of with a huge valleywide project.

Most farmers in the San Joaquin Valley are not enthusiastic about the master drain project. They know that they might have to pay as much as $75 per acre per year as their share of the costs. Farmers with no drainage problems resent having to pay for those who do. But the saline groundwater continues to rise. Crop yields, already declining, will drop further if no action is taken.

Southern Californians seem determined to have water troubles, more of their own making than of nature's.

8. Solutions

Severe water shortages are predicted for the Southwest by 1990 or sooner. Since irrigated agriculture takes such a large share of available water, it will bear the brunt of shortages. So agribusiness interests in particular continue to seek new water supplies.

Their greatest fantasy, revived in a 1981 *Scientific American* article, is called the North American Water and Power Alliance. First proposed in 1964, this project would be by far the greatest attempt to direct water from one region to others. Most of the water would come from Canada—from the headwaters of the Yukon and Tanana rivers and from the Fraser and Peace rivers. Dams in some river valleys would create the Rocky Mountain Trench, a 500-mile reservoir, mostly in British Columbia and Alberta.

Some water from this reservoir would be diverted to eastern Canada and the Upper Mississippi. South of the Rocky Mountain Trench, more water would enter the system from the Snake, the Salmon, and other northwestern rivers in the United States. Millions of acre-feet would be sent to the southwestern states and to Mexico. The cost of the project was estimated at $200 billion in 1964. One attractive feature of this plan—some say the only one—is its hydroelectric potential. Generating plants at dams could produce electricity for all project pumping needs, plus a surplus of up to 70,000 megawatts—equal to one quarter of the average electric production for all power plants in the United States.

This huge project would produce 160 million acre-feet of water. It would be a terrific boon to the Southwest, where millions of acres of additional fertile land could be cultivated if water was available. Of course, the project would not actually produce any water. It would *divert* those acre-feet of water from present uses in Alaska, Canada, and the Northwest, from people, businesses, communities, and wildlife that now rely on the water. This engineering scheme did not take such matters into account, nor did it consider the destruction of wilderness areas, or the question of Canada's cooperation.

Soon after this plan was proposed, a senator from Utah said, "It is not only feasible, it is almost inevitable." In 1980, however, political scientist Thane Gustafson wrote, "Now, after 15 years of environmental legislation and litigation, such a project could sooner be built on the moon than in the United States or Canada."

Proposals of this sort are not confined to the West. If Long Island residents succeed in polluting their great groundwater reserves, an alternate source has been suggested: damming about half of Long Island Sound and turning it into a fresh-water lake. Two dams, one eight miles long, would accomplish this. Fed by the Connecticut River and other fresh-water streams, the lake would eventually hold 42 million acre-feet of fresh water. This plan will face enormous economic and environmental obstacles if it ever reaches the status of a serious proposal.

Nearly all such projects involve building expensive structures, but one proposal does not: towing icebergs up from

This Arctic iceberg is tiny compared with Antarctic icebergs, which may reach ten miles in length.

the Antarctic. This appeals especially to irrigators in southern California and the Lower Colorado Basin, since an iceberg could be parked offshore and its fresh water pumped inland. The idea was first proposed in 1957 and has since been studied by the Rand Corporation, under a grant from the National Science Foundation. Though California is closer to the Arctic than to Antarctica, icebergs from the Antarctic are ten times more abundant and better shaped for towing.

Some of the flat-topped Antarctic icebergs are ten miles long and 900 feet deep. At the most economical towing speed, about a year would be needed to bring an iceberg to southern California. The Rand study envisioned a train of icebergs up

123

to fifty miles long. A plastic covering would reduce melting during the journey. Once at its destination, the iceberg could be used gradually, as ice was removed, melted, and the water pumped inland. The environmental effects of icebergs on aquatic life and local climatic conditions offshore southern California have not been investigated.

In 1977, engineers at the First International Conference on Iceberg Utilization concluded that the problems were formidable. Nevertheless, the idea may be tested on a small iceberg in a few years. It would probably be towed to Saudi Arabia, since that nation's need for fresh water is particularly acute. Saudi Arabia has no lakes or streams and receives only about four inches of rain a year. It obtains water from aquifers and from desalinization. Although the energy costs of towing icebergs would be great, water from them is estimated to be 30 to 50 percent cheaper than that from desalinization. This might be a boost for Saudi Arabia, but it would still be too costly for most uses in the United States. As for desalinization, there are now more than 335 plants in the United States. Most are in California, Texas, and Florida. They produce almost 100 million gallons a day, largely for industrial purposes. Desalinization remains an energy-intensive, expensive way to obtain fresh water.

Weather modification or cloud seeding has been explored as a way to increase water supplies in the arid West. The Bureau of Reclamation's experimental program, called Project Skywater, had some success in the 1970s when winter clouds over southwestern Colorado were seeded with silver iodide crystals. It appeared that snowfall increased, and this may have added to the spring flow of the Colorado River. Research continues, but cloud seeding is believed to be too experimental at this time to be relied on for increased water. Besides, legal problems may prevent its implementation in the United States.

Cloud-seeding to stimulate rain or snow may never get beyond the experimental stage.

Residents in southwestern Colorado were upset about the twelve feet of snow that Project Skywater apparently brought to their streets. At another time and place, people might legitimately claim that cloud seeding robbed them of their normal snow supply.

USING LESS WATER

Faced with the prospect of no new water sources and increasing competition for the natural supplies, agribusinesses see a grim future: "Take our water away and you'll be taking billions of dollars of food from the tables of people all over the United States."

This view is not shared by most agricultural experts. There is abundant evidence that the same or greater food production can be achieved in the arid West with much less water. And there is no doubt that cuts in water use should be aimed at irrigators. Suppose every household in California managed to cut its water use by 75 percent. This would reduce the total water use in the state by only 6.75 percent. The same savings could be achieved if irrigators used just 8 percent less water. Thus a small cutback by irrigators has the same effect as a drastic cutback by city dwellers.

In 1976, the General Accounting Office, which conducts studies for Congress, estimated that more than half of all irrigation water is wasted. The most wasteful methods—flooding whole fields or the furrows between rows—are still widely practiced. At best, half of the water reaches crop roots. With sprinkler irrigation, up to 70 percent of the water reaches the root zones of crop plants. Drip irrigation, in which pipes or plastic hoses deliver drops of water directly to the base of plants, is the most efficient. Up to 90 percent of the water reaches the root zone. (It can be applied to orchards and to most row crops but not to crops planted all over a field, such as rice, wheat, or alfalfa.) Buying equipment for either of these methods is a major expense, so field and furrow flooding continue to be popular in much of the arid West.

Drip irrigation is common in Israel. Measuring devices are used to tell when root zones need water and when they have enough. This enables irrigators to cut water use by half or more. It also has had the surprising effect of increasing crop yields. In one test, a region using sprinklers had yielded nine and a half tons of melons per acre. With drip irrigation it produced more than seventeen tons per acre. Similar results have been reported from California. One farmer experienced a 30 percent greater yield of strawberries while using 55 percent less water. Since little water is lost in drip irrigation, fewer weeds survive between rows, so weed control is less of a problem.

Installation of a drip irrigation system usually costs more than $1,000 an acre. In the West it has been applied first to berries, citrus, grapes, and other crops that yield a high profit per acre. But even irrigators who use the ancient field-flooding methods can cut water use by 25 percent if they use sensing devices to measure soil moisture. Such devices and drip irrigation systems will no longer seem like luxuries when water itself becomes more of a luxury.

Any assessment of western irrigation practices should consider the *kinds* of crops as well as the ways of applying water. "If conserving water is a goal," wrote Marc Reisner of the Natural Resources Defense Council, "then it is absurd to grow rice in arid California, when acreage is available to grow it in Louisiana or Mississippi . . . but rice is grown in California, plenty of it."

Besides rice, alfalfa is commonly grown on irrigated land in the Southwest. It, too, requires large amounts of water. It, too, need not be grown on arid lands. Under ordinary market conditions, water-consuming crops like these would be mostly grown in regions having abundant rainfall. They are being grown in the driest part of the United States because water is often priced at about 10 percent of its actual cost of delivery. Cheap water allows arid lands to compete with regions where water is delivered abundantly by rain.

When Congress created the Bureau of Reclamation in 1902, it deliberately aimed to provide the West with cheap water. Its goal was to promote settlement and economic development. That goal has been accomplished. The arid West no longer needs favored treatment; in fact, it is being harmed by the availability of underpriced water. By using water inefficiently,

A drip irrigation system being installed among newly planted
citrus trees.

it is producing less food and fiber than it can. A 1978 study
by the Rand Corporation concluded that California alone was
losing between $60 million and $370 million annually through
the extravagant use of water.

Allowing water prices to rise is not as simple as it might
seem. Contracts on federal water projects run for forty years.
Nothing can be done to raise prices for water users until the
contracts expire, as some do in the 1980s. The main difficulty,
though, is the tangle of western water laws that affect how
water is used. Under present laws in most western states, waste
of water is encouraged because a person or corporation owning
water rights must use the water or risk losing the rights. The

128

Though expensive to install, drip irrigation systems greatly reduce water use and increase yields of food.

rights can be sold, but usually surplus water cannot. If irrigators could arrange to sell their unneeded water to others, enough water might be freed to eliminate the need for dams and other expensive projects, at least for a while. Such a program would have to include strict limits on groundwater use, however, or this common supply would be greedily pumped for sale.

The federal government, which has done so much to encourage water waste, could play a decisive role in promoting water conservation. It could, for example, withhold new federal funds for water projects until states controlled groundwater pumping and instituted water-saving irrigation methods.

This would undoubtedly be good for the basic water and soil resources of the nation, but such federal intrusion in so-called states' rights was discouraged by the conservative Reagan administration.

Higher water prices are inevitable, and they will bring great change to the arid West. They will induce more western cities to treat waste water, which most discard after one use. The Los Angeles region recycles only 60,000 acre-feet a year out of a potentially reusable 555,000 acre-feet. Hardest hit by higher water costs will be farmers of poor-quality land or those raising low-value crops. Some will go out of business. This will not necessarily harm the region's economy, because the losses may be offset by gains from more efficient use of water on more fertile land. The farming of low-value crops may shift eastward, being unable to compete for costly water with high-value crops, cities, and industries. As they say in the West, "Water ordinarily flows downhill, except when it flows uphill toward money."

High water prices will cause painful adjustments, but they will be less painful than the effects of unchecked continuation of the cheap water era. If irrigators do not stop squandering water, severe shortages lie ahead that will affect every sector of the West's economy and possibly cause a shift of business and population to areas with greater water supplies. "We like the Sun Belt," said a Phoenix businessman, "but we need to be able to count on water as we grow. If this water situation doesn't improve, we will have to consider moving back East."

Easterners pay more for water than westerners. In 1978, 1,000 cubic feet (about 7,500 gallons) cost $4.55 in Los Angeles. The same amount cost $8.90 in Boston and $13.38 in Philadelphia. Still, water is underpriced everywhere, and higher rates in the East will stimulate conservation while providing some of funds needed to remove impurities and to repair deteriorating water systems. Present rates are set too low to keep water systems in good repair or to improve them. Providing enough money for such needs may require rates to rise from 50 to 300 percent in urban areas, according to Steven Hanke, a water economics expert on the President's Council of Economic Advisors.

Raising water prices is considered to be politically unpopular, but growing public awareness of threats to water supplies may make the costs more palatable. There's nothing like a sharp increase in the cost of a resource—either water or energy—to stimulate conservation. Water metering of individual households is an essential element of this effort, of course. Simply installing meters, with increasing rates for increasing amounts used, rather than a flat fee, caused consumption in Boulder, Colorado, to drop 36 percent. The installation of meters may eliminate the need for the expansion of water storage and pumping facilities.

Community water conservation efforts in California, Illinois, and Maryland show that water users can reduce consumption from 38 to 68 percent. During the 1976–1977 drought in California, the worst effects were felt in Marin County, north of San Francisco. The price of water rose more than 300 percent in two years. Household consumption dropped from 122 gallons a day in 1975 to 35 gallons a day in 1977. Water prices were cut back somewhat after the drought, and water-saving efforts also slackened, but, in 1979, people were still using 25 percent less water than they had used before the drought. The manager of the Marin water district said, "We learned that the cheapest, best, quickest way to get more water is to conserve what we have."

People all over the nation have discovered that their water-saving efforts often have an unpleasant side effect: increased water rates. Effective conservation means lower revenues for

Shower flow restrictors reduce both the amount of water used and the fuel needed to heat water.

water companies, which have certain fixed costs of operation. So rates go up and customers feel they are being punished for their water-saving efforts. However, conservation has also enabled some communities to defer expensive projects that would have added much more to water bills.

Bathing and toilet flushing represent half of all household water use, and showers and toilets can be easily adapted to use less water. People who put flow restrictors in shower heads usually get a double benefit: Since less hot water is used, both water and fuel bills drop. The flush toilet is criticized as a major cause of water supply and water pollution problems. Most toilets now on the market in the United States use about three and a half gallons of water with each flush, but older toilets already installed use between five and six gallons per flush. In a year's time, each person uses about 9,000 gallons of water to remove just 165 gallons of waste. Then large amounts of money are spent to separate this small fraction of waste so that the water can be used again.

There are alternatives, including toilets that use less water or no water (vacuum-flushed) and even some that retain wastes and convert them to safe, odorless garden compost. A few hundred composting toilets are now used in the United States. They are likely to remain rare, because most people would prefer water-saving toilets that resemble the ones they're used to. If most households had toilets that use just two quarts of water per flush, water use in urban areas would drop dramatically.

Water supplies could also be stretched by creating dual or plural water systems. In present single systems, the finest-quality drinking water is used to flush toilets, wash cars, and water lawns. It is used because only one grade of water is available. A plural water supply system would offer two or more grades. The best water would be used only for drinking, cooking, and bathing. Lower-quality water would fulfill the great bulk of water uses. A dual system would greatly reduce the cost of supplying drinking water (since much less of this high-grade water would be needed). The cost of treating waste water would also lessen. Installing such a system would mean running a new set of pipes to each household—a formidable job in older cities. In a new development, however, a dual water supply would cost only about 20 percent more than a single supply.

The idea of dual water systems has scarcely been considered

in the United States, and only a tiny fraction of homes have modern two-quart-flush toilets. A larger but still small fraction of households have flow restrictors in shower heads. Drip irrigation is practiced on less than 1 percent of all irrigated farmland in the United States. Clearly, we have not begun to discover how much water we can save.

In both East and West, the answer to safe, dependable water supplies does not lie in such glamorous projects as huge dams or icebergs hauled up from Antarctica. It lies in such mundane projects as plugging leaks in city water pipes and in irrigation canals, in such devices as soil-moisture sensors and water flow restrictors, and especially in human ingenuity to make every drop of water count.

The conservation and reuse of water might be called the last water hole. It will be as pure and as deep as we want to make it.

Glossary

AGRIBUSINESS—the business of agriculture, especially that part controlled by large corporations which are usually absentee owners (in contrast to small, family-owned and -operated farms).

AQUIFER—an underground formation of porous rocks, loose sands, gravels, or soils where water collects.

CARCINOGEN—a substance or other factor (such as radioactive particles or ultraviolet rays from the sun) which causes cancerous cells to grow.

COAL-LIQUEFACTION—the process of converting solid coal to liquid methanol or gasoline. To achieve this, coal is enriched with hydrogen under pressure at high temperatures.

DESALINIZATION—the process of removing salts from sea water or from fresh water that has a high salt content. In one modern process, called reverse osmosis, water is forced through a plastic membrane that blocks most of the salt.

ESTUARY—a place where salt water and fresh water mix, usually where ocean tides enter a river. Estuaries are usually called bays, sounds, harbors, or lagoons.

HYDROELECTRICITY—electricity produced by using the energy of flowing or falling water to turn turbine generators.

HYDROLOGIST—a scientist who studies the properties, distribution, and effects of water on the earth's surface, beneath the surface, and in the atmosphere.

LEACH—to filter out soluble chemicals from a substance. Rain water may leach toxic chemicals from landfills into streams, lakes, aquifers, and other sources of drinking water.

OIL SHALE—a fine-grained sedimentary rock which contains an oil-yielding substance called kerogen. The best oil shale in the United States yields less than thirty gallons of oil from a ton of rock.

ORGANIC CHEMICALS—chemicals which contain carbon compounds. They include such chemical groups as alcohols, ethers, esters, and aldehydes.

PETROCHEMICALS—compounds of mostly carbon and hydrogen, made by chemical conversion of natural gas, petroleum, or oil refinery products. Petrochemicals include ammonia, acetylene, ethylene, benzene, toluene, naphthalene, and are found in thousands of items used by consumers.

RADIOACTIVITY—behavior of a substance in which the nuclei of atoms undergo change and emit radiation in the form of alpha particles, beta particles, or gamma rays. About fifty elements, including uranium, are naturally radioactive.

SYNTHETIC FUELS—gas or liquid fuels produced from coal, oil shale, tar sands, or other materials. They are not literally synthetic (which means something entirely human-made and artificial), but are naturally occurring fossil fuels converted into more convenient forms of energy.

VIRUSES—the smallest, simplest forms of life, which are able to reproduce only within the cells of a living thing.

WATERSHED—the area from which water drains into a pond, lake, stream, or river. A pond may have a watershed of a few acres, while the watershed of a large river may consist of millions of acres. Watersheds are also called drainage basins or basins.

WATER TABLE—the top level of groundwater. In low areas the water table reaches the surface and contributes (along with runoff of rain and melted snow) to the water of ponds, marshes, and rivers. Drought or excessive pumping of groundwater from wells causes the water table to drop.

Further Reading

AMBROGGI, ROBERT, "Water." *Scientific American,* September 1980, pp. 100-116.

AUCOIN, JAMES, "The Irrigation Revolution." *Environment,* October 1979, pp. 17-20, 38-40.

BOSLOUGH, JOHN, "Rationing a River." *Science 81,* June 1981, pp. 26-27.

BOWDEN, CHARLES, *Killing the Hidden Waters.* Austin: University of Texas Press, 1977.

CANBY, THOMAS, "Water: Our Most Precious Resource." *National Geographic,* August 1980, pp. 144-179.

CAVANAGH, RALPH, "The Pacific Northwest is Praying for Rain." *The Amicus Journal,* Summer 1980, pp. 31-38.

CHASAN, DANIEL, "Mono Lake vs. Los Angeles: A Tug-of-War for Precious Water." *Smithsonian,* April 1981, pp. 42-50.

DENNIS, HARRY, *Water and Power: The Peripheral Canal and Its Alternatives.* San Francisco: Friends of the Earth, 1981.

EGGINGTON, JOYCE, "The Long Island Lesson." *Audubon,* July 1981, pp. 84-93.

FRAZIER, KENDRICK, "Is There an Iceberg in Your Future?" *Science News,* November 5, 1977, pp. 298-300.

HELLMAN, HAL, "The Day New York Runs Out of Water." *Science 81,* May 1981, pp. 72-75.

KASPERSON, ROGER, ed., *Water Re-Use and the Cities.* Worcester, Mass.: Clark University Press, 1977.

KEOUGH, CAROL, *Water Fit to Drink.* Emmaus, Pa.: Rodale Press, Inc., 1980.

LOVE, SAM, "An Idea in Need of Rethinking: The Flush Toilet." *Smithsonian,* May 1975, pp. 61-66.

PILLSBURY, ARTHUR, "The Salinity of Rivers." *Scientific American*, July 1981, pp. 54-65.

POLSGROVE, CAROL, "In Hot Water: Uranium Mining and Water Pollution." *Sierra*, November-December 1980, pp. 28-31.

REISNER, MARC, "Dry Times in the Big City." *Geo*, July 1981, pp. 90-111.

RICHARDS, BILL, "The Untamed Yellowstone." *National Geographic*, August 1981, pp. 257-278.

ROBERTS, RICHARD, "Don't Call It 'the Barrens'." *Audubon*, July 1981, pp. 72-83.

RUSSELL, CLIFFORD, ed., *Safe Drinking Water: Current and Future Problems*. Baltimore: Johns Hopkins University Press, 1978.

SHERIDAN, DAVID, "The Desert Blooms—At a Price." *Environment*, April 1981, pp. 6-20, 38-41.

———, "The Underwatered West." *Environment*, March 1981, pp. 6-13, 30-33.

SIBLEY, GEORGE, "The Desert Empire." *Harper's*, October 1977, pp. 49-68.

STEINHART, PETER, "The City and the Inland Sea." *Audubon*, September 1980, pp. 98-125.

U.S. WATER RESOURCES COUNCIL, *The Nation's Water Resources, 1975-2000*. Washington, D.C.: U.S. Government Printing Office, 1978.

VITULLO–MARTIN, JULIA, "Ending the Southwest's Water Binge." *Fortune*, February 23, 1981, pp. 93-104.

WALSH, JOHN, "What to Do When the Well Runs Dry." *Science*, November 14, 1980, pp. 754-756.

WARREN, JACQUELINE, "Water, Water Everywhere." *The Amicus Journal*, Summer 1981, pp. 15-21.

YOUNG, GORDON, "The Troubled Waters of Mono Lake." *National Geographic*, October 1981, pp. 504-519.

Index

141

INDEX

144